Best Practices for Shared Parishes

So That They May All Be One

I0806626

Committee on Cultural Diversity in the Church
UNITED STATES CONFERENCE OF CATHOLIC BISHOPS
WASHINGTON, DC

Our Sunday Visitor
Huntington, Indiana

The document *Best Practices for Shared Parishes: So That They May All Be One* was developed as a resource by the Committee on Cultural Diversity in the Church of the United States Conference of Catholic Bishops (USCCB). It was reviewed by the committee chairman, Bishop Daniel Flores, and has been authorized for publication by the undersigned.

Msgr. Ronny Jenkins
General Secretary, USCCB

Illustrations on pages 10, 13, and 17 by Carmen Fernández.

Cover Image, "Jesus the Word," copyright © 2014 Michele Hehenberger, courtesy of Das Grup, Inc. Used with permission. All rights reserved.

Excerpt from Pope John Paul II, *Ecclesia in America*, copyright © 1999, Libreria Editrice Vaticana (LEV); excerpt from Pope Francis, Homily, March 14, 2013, copyright © 2013, LEV. All rights reserved.

Excerpts from the *Code of Canon Law: Latin-English Edition, New English Translation* copyright © 1998, Canon Law Society of America, Washington, DC, are reprinted with permission.

Scripture excerpts used in this work are taken from the *New American Bible*, rev. ed. © 2010, 1991, 1986, 1970 Confraternity of Christian Doctrine, Inc., Washington, DC. All rights reserved. No part of this work may be reproduced or transmitted in any form or by any means, electronic or mechanical, including photocopying, recording, or by any information storage and retrieval system, without permission in writing from the copyright owner.

Copyright © 2013, United States Conference of Catholic Bishops, Washington, DC. All rights reserved. No part of this work may be reproduced or transmitted in any form or by any means, electronic or mechanical, including photocopying, recording, or by any information storage and retrieval system, without permission in writing from the copyright holder.

ISBN 978-1-63966-141-1 (Inventory No. T2855)
First printing, February 2014
Digital edition, June 2021
Current printing, 2023, published by OSV. Our Sunday VIsitor, Inc., 200 Noll Plaza, Huntington, IN 46750; www.osv.com; 1-800-348-2440

Printed in the United States of America

Contents

Contenido

Best Practices for Shared Parishes: So That They May All Be One

Acknowledgments: We thank the twenty pastors who contributed their time, knowledge, and experience to the elaboration of this resource for parish ministry. Their pastoral sensitivity and practical recommendations are the foundation for this guide. Moreover, their apostolic zeal and ability to bring people from different cultures and ethnicities together as one parish faith community is a true inspiration for pastors and parish leaders across the United States of America. We also thank Carmen Aguinaco for bringing together the experiences and contributions of the pastors, and Brett C. Hoover, PhD, for developing the working document that served as the foundation for this guide. In a special way we thank Rev. Stephen Dudek, Rev. Michael Johnson, OFM, and Rev. Hector Madrigal for accompanying the development of the guide from its beginning stages to its final articulation.

Background: In 2007, the Catholic bishops of the United States made cultural diversity in the Church one of the top five priorities of their strategic plan, in order to better respond to the growing reality across parishes and dioceses in the United States of America. The USCCB task group working on this priority recommended the development of a practical guide to assist pastors of culturally diverse parishes in the challenging task of building unity in diversity. Such a guide was considered important and urgent since the number of parishes shared by culturally diverse communities had grown dramatically in the previous decade, going from 22 percent in 2000 to 33 percent in 2010.

The Committee on Cultural Diversity in the Church was asked to play a key role in developing the guide, through consultation with pastors who have successfully achieved a high level of ecclesial integration/inclusion among their culturally diverse parishioners. Twenty pastors from different ethnic backgrounds and regions of the country were consulted over a period of eighteen months. Final recommendations for the guide were made in December 2012, including the title *Best Practices for Shared Parishes: So That They May All Be One*.

The term "shared parishes" describes parish communities in which two or more languages or cultural contexts are present in the ministerial life of a parish. The term was coined by Brett Hoover and has been adopted for use in this guide.

Purpose: The purpose of the guide is to assist pastors of shared parishes and their teams in achieving a high level of ecclesial integration among their culturally diverse members. It is designed as a practical tool to (a) assess challenging ministerial situations in light of Catholic pastoral principles and values, (b) identify pastoral responses to address ministerial situations based on proven best practices, (c) apply intercultural competencies in the form of attitudes, knowledge, and skills, and (d) discern pastoral planning strategies based on a developmental process of ecclesial integration/inclusion and intercultural sensitivity, which lead to a higher level of stewardship.

Methodology: The guide has three parts. The first part describes the six stages of intercultural sensitivity developed by Milton Bennett and how they apply to a parish faced with the challenge of responding to demographic changes within its boundaries. Part I illustrates how a pastor and his staff may go through different stages of understanding their mission as they seek to respond to a new reality. Bennett's stages of intercultural sensitivity describe how facing demographic changes may include going through a process of denial, defensiveness, and minimizing the emerging cultural diversity in our midst before moving into a process of accepting, adapting, and integrating that new reality. Part I also includes pastoral experiences that illustrate best practices from some of the shared parishes that participated in the consultation.

Part II articulates the Catholic understanding of the parish and the pastoral principles and values that guide the Catholic parish's life and mission. This understanding moves our reflection from the sociological implications of cultural diversity into the mission of the Catholic Church framed in canon law and guided by the Church's deepest identity, namely, its mission to evangelize.

It also reflects on the ministerial spirituality of the pastor and his team as they respond to the challenges of growing cultural diversity in the spirit of the New Evangelization. The Christian methodology of encounter with the living Jesus Christ as the way to conversion, communion, and solidarity, articulated in the Apostolic Exhortation *Ecclesia in America*, provides the framework for Part II.

Part III offers a three-threshold roadmap that illustrates how parishes have been successful in building unity in diversity among their culturally diverse members. These thresholds are *welcoming, belonging,* and *ownership*. They describe the developmental process for ecclesial integration/inclusion we want to achieve in the growing number of shared parishes "so that they may all be one" (Jn 17:21). The three thresholds for ecclesial integration/inclusion are described through nine movements or indicators. Then the movements are illustrated in real ministerial situations that have been successfully addressed by pastors and their teams. The pastors who participated in the consultation agreed that a higher level of ecclesial integration/inclusion among all parishioners results in a higher level of stewardship and mission.

Developmental Movements or Indicators: The guide offers nine developmental indicators or movements as keys to measure the level of ecclesial integration/inclusion in a particular shared parish and to discern next steps. They include pastoral principles and intercultural competencies relevant to the level of ecclesial integration/inclusion called forth in each movement. The first three movements are integral to the threshold of the sense of *welcoming*. Movements 4, 5, and 6 are the fruit of the sense of *belonging*. Movements 7, 8, and 9 are an expression of the sense of *ownership*.

Welcoming

- Mission
- Homecoming
- Ministerial Growth

Belonging

- Build Relationships Across Cultures
- Intercultural Leadership Development and Formation
- Decision-Making Process

Ownership

- Sharing Resources
- Achieving Stewardship
- Communion in Mission

How to Use This Guide: This guide can be used as a tool to train parish staff and leaders in the process of ecclesial integration/inclusion.

Part I focuses on the stages of intercultural sensitivity. It aims at helping parish staff and leaders assess their level of intercultural sensitivity and how can they move forward in such a process. It may be helpful to provide data on the demographics of the parish as a good starting point for the session. Part II can be conducted in a retreat fashion in order to maximize the benefits of such rich spiritual content. The spirituality of hospitality and reconciliation are quite central to Part II, as it touches on matters of personal encounter, conversion, communion, and solidarity in Christ.

Part III can be presented as a developmental process to assess two different realities. One is the level of ecclesial integration/inclusion that the parish has achieved so far. Another is the level of intercultural competency that each staff member and parish leader has mastered in terms of attitudes, knowledge, and skills.

The training can be done in multiple forms. For example, it can be done as a one-day in-service or in a series of three evenings, dedicating one evening to each part of the guide.

The guide can also be used as a pastoral planning tool to help discern the next steps a particular parish should take on its way to becoming more interculturally competent and better integrated, in the Catholic sense of the word.

PART I

Shared Parishes and Intercultural Sensitivity

What are shared parishes and how do they become so? The term "shared parishes" describes parish communities in which two or more languages or cultural contexts are an integral part of the ministerial life and mission of a particular parish. An example of a shared parish is St. Camillus Parish in Silver Spring, Maryland, where the Sunday Liturgy is celebrated in English, French, and Spanish, as well as in the cultural and spiritual context of the African American community. These four distinct ethnic/cultural communities share together in the life and mission of one parish community. Religious education, youth ministry, and other ministries are also offered in different languages, but they are organized and coordinated under one vision for religious education, youth ministry, and so on. St. Camillus Parish has been a shared parish for a number of years and has achieved a high degree of ecclesial integration through a commonly shared Catholic identity. However, that was not always the case. For many years St. Camillus served a rather homogeneous community of mostly well-established Catholics of European heritage. It was a change in demographics that challenged St. Camillus's pastor and his team to respond to the growing culturally diverse groups living within the parish boundaries.

Today, 33 percent of parishes in the United States are shared parishes compared with 22 percent in the year 2000. The number of shared parishes is expected to grow significantly in the foreseeable future as demographic changes continue to take place, mostly due to the influx of new Catholic immigrants from the Southern Hemisphere. The consolidation of parishes is another factor behind the growing number of shared parishes.

Transitioning from a culturally homogeneous parish to a shared parish is not an easy task. A sense of uncertainty, fear of the unknown, a sense of scarcity, limited intercultural competence, and a certain tendency to want to assimilate people into being "like us" are some of the factors that keep parishioners from embracing fellow Catholics from different cultures and ethnicities. The tendency to view the parish as a congregation rather than a territory, as defined in canon law, is also a hindrance.

Six Stages of Intercultural Sensitivity

A number of pastors who participated in the consultation to develop this guide referred to Milton Bennett's six stages of intercultural sensitivity as a helpful tool to understand what pastors and their teams may go through as they struggle to respond to demographic changes. The six stages are denial, defense, minimizing, acceptance, adaptation, and integration, and they describe how a person or an organization goes from resisting engaging people from a different culture to being open and able to work, relate, and collaborate with culturally diverse populations. The stages are also helpful for pastors and staff already ministering in shared parishes who may find themselves stuck at one point or another in the developmental process of ecclesial integration/inclusion.

The following is an example of a traditionally culturally homogeneous parish going through the above mentioned stages of intercultural sensitivity. The example shows a neighborhood where the number of new Haitian immigrants has grown significantly within the geographical boundaries of the parish. The pastor/administrator and the staff are not aware of this growing presence and have no experience working with Haitian immigrants.

Stage 1. Denial

The pastor is asked about the presence of new Haitian immigrants in his parish. The pastor answers by saying: *We don't have Haitians in the parish.* He adds that there are a few Haitian families but *they are just like everybody else and have been parishioners for a long time.* The pastor and his staff are very surprised when they hear that data from the 2010 Census show more than three hundred Haitian families living within the parish boundaries. Denial may persist on the part of the pastor and/or staff, who may argue that these people are just passing through, that they are not necessarily Catholic, or that they may be "illegals." In the denial stage people tend not to see the "other" or to consider the "other" as somebody else's responsibility.

Stage 2. Defense

Once the pastor and his staff have become aware of the presence of a community of Catholics who are not being reached out to or included, there is a tendency to rationalize why "these people" are not included. Reasons given may include some of the following arguments: *We have no more room in this parish. Can they be trusted? They are going to take over! They are not like us, my grandparents built this parish. They should go to the next parish.* These reasons are often motivated by fear of the unknown. They are not necessarily intended to be harmful or racist, but they are often motivated by stereotypes and can come across as discriminatory.

Stage 3. Minimizing

The pastor and his team are aware of the significant number of Haitian families living within the parish boundaries, and they recognize it is the parish's responsibility to respond. However, there is a move to minimize differences in order not to change the way things are done in the parish. For instance, arguments in this stage usually go something like this: *They can participate if they want to, the door is wide open;* or *They live in America now and should learn English and assimilate like everybody else.* This response begins to show a degree of openness to welcoming people, but only as long as things don't change in "our parish" and they leave their language, culture, traditions, and expectations at the door. The expression "color-blind" fits here in the literal sense, as people choose not to see the differences with the other. However, the intent is to justify not having to do anything different, but waiting for the other to fit into "our" way of thinking and "our" way of doing things. Establishing the Sunday Liturgy in Creole is considered unnecessary and can even be considered divisive. This stage is particularly difficult to overcome when it comes to faith formation of children and young people of new immigrant populations. The fact that children of immigrants know English, or are in the process of learning it, leaves significant differences out of the equation such as culture, race, educational attainment, economic and social status, and immigration status, among others.

Stage 4. Acceptance

In this stage the pastor and the staff recognize differences as quite real and know that the same behavior may mean different things for people of different cultures. There is a willingness to shift perspective while still maintaining a commitment to "our own values." Establishing the Sunday Liturgy in Creole may be fine if they don't disturb others and take good care of "our things." In this stage the well-established community and the new Haitian community may share the same buildings, parking lot, and church building, but at different times, avoiding each other. A sacramental minister from another parish is likely to preside at the Sunday Liturgy in Creole with very little contact with the pastor and his staff. There is a sense of treating each other politely, but the "us"/"them" language prevails.

Stage 5. Adaptation

In the adaptation stage, the pastor and his staff are able to understand and empathize with different perspectives, and adapt their behavior accordingly. The pastor, his staff, and the leadership of the immigrant community have developed significant intercultural competencies such as the ability to communicate in two languages, establishing interpersonal relationships across cultures, and openness to new ideas and projects originating in either community. There is a sense that both communities belong together in the parish and that people are more willing to relate, work, and collaborate with one another. The "we" language is used among the leadership in both communities. There are a variety of programs and projects available in both languages, and changes have been made to accommodate the needs of the Haitian community within certain limits. Moving the Sunday Liturgy in Creole to a better time or allowing fund-raising activities for specific Haitian programs and activities are significant changes in parish life. However, at this stage there is still not a great deal of participation by the immigrant community in decision-making bodies like the parish council, the financial council, or the staff.

Stage 6. Integration

At this stage the pastor, his team, and the leadership of the Haitian community move quite naturally from one cultural framework to the other, adapting to different situations with ease and cultural accuracy. The leadership in both cultural communities has a sense of ownership in the parish. There is a good representation of both cultures in all decision-making bodies and in the parish staff, and resources are generated and shared according to the needs and aspirations of both communities in the parish.

The Three Areas of Intercultural Competence

Developing intercultural sensitivity requires the acquisition of intercultural competence for ministry. Intercultural competence is the capacity to communicate, relate, and work across cultural boundaries. It involves developing capacity in three areas: *knowledge, skills,* and *attitudes.*

INTERCULTURAL COMPETENCIES

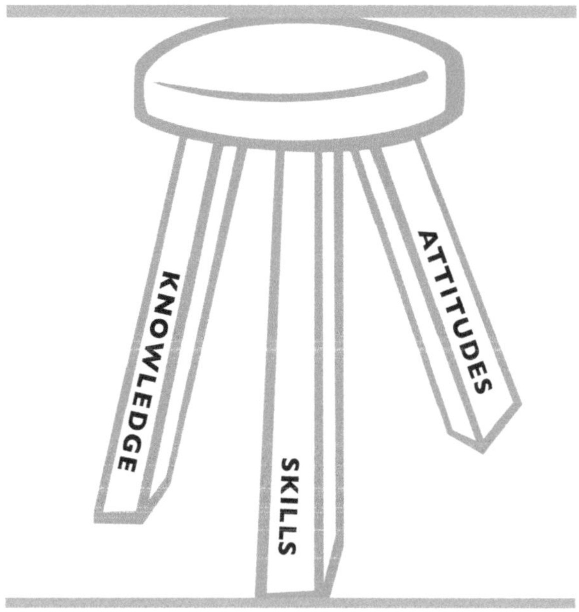

Knowledge involves the capacity to understand more than one perspective on how things are done. Knowing how different cultural communities make decisions, how they use time during their meetings, how far ahead they plan, how they raise funds for the parish, how they go about preparing and celebrating the liturgy, etc., allows the intercultural minister to facilitate communication, organization, and implementation of common parish activities. *Knowledge* favors the "both-and" approach over the "one-size-fits-all" approach.

Skills include the ability to communicate in more than one language, to empathize with parishioners from different cultures and lived realities, to be a good listener, and to motivate people to actively engage in the various ministries of the parish. They also include the capacity to facilitate meetings, conduct trainings, coordinate volunteers, deal with conflict, and provide support to leaders from different cultures. *Skills* make of the minister an "intercultural mentor" who knows how to "plan with people, not for people."

Attitudes include openness to engage parishioners from different cultures with a sense of gratitude and curiosity. It makes people feel at home and is effective in building relationships across cultures that lead to mutual acceptance, appreciation, and collaboration. *Attitudes* describe a minister as a "bridge-builder" who brings people together and invites their unique gifts for the good of all and the common mission of the parish.

Consider the following questions to see where you and the leadership in your parish are on the continuum of intercultural sensitivity and in the area of intercultural competence:

a) Has your parish experienced a significant demographic shift in the past few years?
b) How has your parish responded to this population shift?
c) What stage of intercultural sensitivity best describes where you and members of your staff are at on this continuum?
d) What intercultural competencies—knowledge, attitudes, and skills—are in use by the pastor, staff, and parish leaders?
e) What aspects are keeping the leadership in the parish from achieving the next stage of intercultural sensitivity or greater intercultural competence?

Stories from the Trenches

The six stages of intercultural sensitivity and the three areas of intercultural competence are quite useful in understanding the process of achieving unity in diversity. The stages are also helpful in identifying benchmarks and competencies as we go through the process. However, when we talk about ministry, both spirituality and a commitment to the good of the human person call for an added dimension of responsibility to one another. Such a dimension comes from the fact that the Church's mission is precisely to bring the Good News of Jesus Christ to every human situation. It also calls us to welcome one another and be custodians of the dignity of every human person, particularly the most vulnerable among us.

The following are stories of shared parishes that have embraced the call to reach out to diverse ethnic/cultural populations living within their boundaries. In some cases the pastors and their teams were aware of the stages of intercultural sensitivity and intercultural competence, and used them to navigate the ambiguous waters of intercultural relations. In some cases they just followed their pastoral intuition and a good degree of common sense and solidarity. However, the ingredient that is very much present in every case is the apostolic zeal on the part of the pastor and his team to fulfill their ecclesial mandate to bring the Good News of Jesus Christ to all ethnic/cultural communities under their pastoral care. After consultation with the pastors of twenty shared parishes, we offer the following snapshots of several well-functioning shared parishes around the country.

St. Francis de Sales Parish sits in a suburban community west of Grand Rapids, Michigan, in a town called Holland. Hispanic, Vietnamese, and American parishioners of European descent all share St. Francis as a spiritual home. In 1995, a fire erupted within the parish church on the Feast of Our Lady of Guadalupe. The worship space was largely destroyed. Before it was to be demolished, the parish engaged in a period of communal mourning. They "waked the church," as then-pastor Fr. Stephen Dudek called it. He remembers, "People came into the burnt space to offer flowers, light candles, and share memories." Next, people from all three communities worked together, side by side, with hammers and chisels to salvage about 10,000 bricks from the ruins, bricks that were eventually incorporated into the rebuilt church. "Reactor groups" were formed from each of the three communities, and they all contributed their ideas to the new design. The rebuilt church contained sacred art from all three of these cultural traditions, and it was constructed in the round to emphasize the equality of all of them.

The parish of St. Joseph in Amarillo, Texas, combines an older, middle-class Mexican American and European American community with younger Hispanic immigrants and refugees from Sudan and Bosnia. When a new pastor, Fr. Hector Madrigal, arrived in 2007, he conducted listening sessions and learned firsthand about many of the divisions within the parish, mostly centered on competition between different local schools, Catholic and public. The listening sessions led to a *covenant* or pact in which all the community groups committed to working toward unity in Christ. They celebrated this covenant with a healing service and then with the parish's first unity Mass outside under a tent. All the different parties of the parish entered the tent in procession and signed the covenant in the presence of the diocesan bishop. Each year, the parish hosts a renewal ceremony with another multilingual unity Mass outdoors. They also honor a "unity in Christ" stone placed near the church entrance to remind everyone of their commitment to one another in God's sight.

St. Camillus in Silver Spring, Maryland, is the kind of shared parish that staggers the imagination of most Catholics. Run by Franciscan friars, the parish is located in the culturally and socioeconomically diverse northern suburbs of the Washington, D.C., metro area. It hosts almost five thousand people each weekend for Mass. The largest group in the parish is the Central American community, mostly from El Salvador and Guatemala. Twenty-five percent of the parishioners are English- and French-speaking new immigrants from Africa, and one fifth are European Americans; there is also an African American community and a community of Bengali people (originally from Bangladesh). Under the leadership of Fr. Michael Johnson, OFM, the parish staff represents all these groups, and Mass is celebrated every Sunday in three languages (Spanish, English, and French). There are trilingual liturgies on six holidays, plus on Christmas and during the Easter Triduum. The Rosary is prayed in five languages every morning. A host of lay ecclesial movements (such as the charismatic renewal movement and the SEARCH retreat movement) have a home at St. Camillus. Parishioners are involved (often together) in seventy-two different ministries including catechesis, evangelization, liturgical and youth ministries, social service and justice organizations, and more. A committee of people also promotes "Care for Creation," or ecological concerns, on Spanish-language radio.

Yuba City is a small city in the agriculturally rich Sacramento Valley of Northern California. Therein is **St. Isidore Parish**. At St. Isidore's, as in much of California, European American people are not the majority group. The parish has four Masses in English and three in Spanish, but those attending in Spanish form a slight majority. Religious education is taught in both languages, using a bilingual book under the direction of a bilingual director of religious education. The parish's St. Francis of Assisi Fund helps poor and homeless people of any background. Twice a year, a hundred or more volunteers from the Hispanic, European American, and Filipino communities join forces to host grand dinners for local homeless people, making it one of many expressions of unity in diversity according to Fr. Francisco Hernandez, pastor of the parish.

Schaumburg, Illinois, is a socioeconomically and culturally diverse outer ring suburb of the Chicago area. **The Church of the Holy Spirit** there welcomes a multicultural community of European Americans, Hispanics (mostly Mexicans), and Filipinos, with a smattering of other immigrants. The parish council conducts open meetings five times a year to ensure all parishioners have a voice in parish affairs. The pastor, Fr. William Tkachuk, attributes the success of the parish to "a willingness on the part of parish leaders among the different ethnic groups to continue to develop and enhance the structures and activities that nourish the parish vision of one Body of Christ with many diverse members," a vision rooted in the unity-in-diversity of the Holy Trinity. The parish actively works for immigrant rights. Yet, Fr. Bill admits that some people do not appreciate the bilingual liturgies that occur on Holy Thursday and other feast days. He recalls a parishioner expressing, "Why do we have to do this in two languages? I just don't like it." The pastor answered, "It is okay not to like it." He frankly acknowledges the difficulty for those who are not bilingual. "But [including the languages of all] is the demand of gospel justice," he adds. "We are not attempting to be politically correct, but to live the Gospel. We do not have to like it to be committed to doing it."

On the other hand, parishioners at **Our Lady of Lourdes** seem to enjoy their occasional bilingual liturgies. Located in Montclair, in the Inland Empire County east of Los Angeles, California, the parish is split into almost equal quarters—Mexican and Central American, South American, European American, and Asian. A year of education around bilingual celebrations helped form a common ethos, summarized in the mission statement: "We embrace the mission of Jesus and seek to build up the body of Christ and to bring all people, all races, and all ethnic groups into full union with Him. We journey together in faith and strive to be a prayerful and Eucharistic family." The pastor, Fr. Anthony Dao, says that regularly inviting different communities to serve one another at various events helps cement the relationships between cultural communities. But he notes that everyone should be cautious about expecting too much too soon.

Finally, as Fr. Stephen Dudek points out, there are issues of diversity and inclusion not just between and among cultures—Latino, Vietnamese, Sudanese, etc.—but also within the broader categories and/or cultural families themselves. He uses as an example the diversity of Latino or Hispanic cultures present within his current parish. At **St. Joseph the Worker**, they have begun celebrating a novena in honor of Our Lady of the Rosary—the title under which the Guatemalan people honor Mary—to go along with the novena in honor of Our Lady of Guadalupe. This, in turn, inspired the Puerto Rican community to breathe new life into their novena to Our Lady Mother of Divine Providence. Also, for the growing Guatemalan portion of the community, a novena was added in January in honor of the *Cristo Negro de Esquipulas*. For the feast of Our Lady of Charity of Cobre—the title by which Cubans honor Mary—they had a Cuban dinner after Mass, and it was the first time most of the Guatemalan parishioners ever had eaten Cuban food. These kinds of interactions within the diverse communities themselves are also important to keep in mind.

QUESTIONS FOR REFLECTION

1) What are some commonalities you find in these shared parishes?
2) What gospel values do you see lifted up?
3) What challenges and opportunities can you identify?
4) In what ways do they inspire you in your ministry?
5) What stage of intercultural sensitivity do you think has been achieved in each parish?

PART II

The Catholic Understanding of the Parish Life and Mission

The Catholic Parish

Based on the feedback received from the pastors involved in the consultation, a significant number of parish staff and leaders view the parish more as a congregation, that is, a group of registered Catholics who are involved to various degrees in the life the parish. Such an understanding of the parish is often based on the experience of well-established Catholic faithful who have known each other for a long time. This congregational view of the parish is more reflective of a uniquely American Protestant faith community that centers Christian life on those who *voluntarily* gather for worship. In contrast, the Catholic Church defines the parish in several different ways that are not mutually exclusive. For example, canon 515 §1 reads, "A parish is a certain community of the Christian faithful stably constituted in a particular church," and canon 518 establishes that "as a general rule a parish is to be territorial, that is, one which includes all the Christian faithful of a certain territory." The latter definition views the parish as a territory with clearly marked geographical boundaries.

According to canon law, the pastor is responsible for the spiritual well-being of all those living within the defined parish boundaries, not only the ones who are "registered." As such, the pastor and his team are called to a constant ministry of mission that strives to bring the Good News of Jesus Christ to every human situation present in the parish. The evangelizing role of the pastor is held up in canon law, as is the missionary nature of the Church. The spiritual welfare of the faithful is an essential element. The call to a New Evangelization makes much more sense when we think of the parish as a territory. All kinds of possibilities and opportunities can be generated by the pastor and his team as they seek new and creative ways to reach out to all baptized Catholics and to others living within the parish boundaries, not only those already gathered.

It is important to note that it is quite acceptable for Catholics to be members of a parish even if they live outside the boundaries of that particular parish. This practice is widely used in the United States and with very good pastoral results. However, this practice does not exempt the responsibility of the pastor and his team from responding to the pastoral needs and aspirations of people living within the boundaries of that parish. We must also remember that some parishes are non-territorial, such as those affiliated with colleges and universities, military facilities, and some ethnic parishes.

Shared parishes present significant challenges, but they offer even greater opportunities to engage in profound conversations about life and faith—opportunities to worship and pray together, to learn from each other, to be there for one another, to forgive one another and be reconciled, to acknowledge our unique histories, and to discover ways in which we can be one Catholic parish, yet come from diverse cultures and ethnicities.

The Call to Ongoing Mission

Today, more than ever, it is paramount for parishes to reclaim their missionary roots and vocation. The growing cultural diversity in thousands of parishes across the United States requires that pastors and their teams go out and meet the newcomers where they are at in their lives. In some cases, it is long-time Catholic residents in a neighborhood that need to be visited with the Good News and invited to active participation in the life and mission of the parish community. The

MISSION

mission of the parish also extends to non-Catholics, particularly the most vulnerable. The work of Catholic Charities and other social ministry Catholic agencies is very important to the mission of the Church. However, each parish benefits from practicing works of mercy directly to people living in the neighborhood. Moreover, the celebration of the sacraments, particularly the Eucharist, the ongoing learning of our Catholic faith, the need for a nurturing prayer life, the call to build up the Church as the beloved community, and the consistent ministry of solidarity with the most vulnerable are all essential dimensions Christian life. All baptized Catholics living in a particular parish need access to the practice of every dimension of their Catholic faith.

How can pastors and their teams reach out to diverse cultural groups present in the parish? How do they know that they are doing things the right way? What should the ultimate goal be in welcoming these communities? How do you achieve unity in diversity among parishioners from different cultures and ethnicities? How do you promote the healthy interaction of new Catholic immigrants in the life of the Church and in U.S. society? Our own history and previous pastoral practices can help us address these and other questions that emerge in the context of shared parishes.

Shared Parishes and the Principle of Ecclesial Integration/Inclusion

In 1999, Blessed Pope John Paul II wrote to the culturally distinct churches of North America and Latin America about the call to unity in diversity in the Apostolic Exhortation *Ecclesia in America*:

> The Church is the sign of communion because her members, like branches, share the life of Christ, the true vine (cf. Jn 15:5). Through communion with Christ, Head of the Mystical Body, we enter into living communion with all believers. This communion, present in the Church and essential to her nature, must be made visible in concrete signs. (no. 33)

The Holy Father saw Catholics in the Americas finding unity through a process of spiritual conversion, followed by concrete signs of communion, and then solidarity with all human beings. Such communion and solidarity are also extended to every culture in the universal Church that embraces the entire human family. In other words, we are concretely changed by the relationships we have with one another in Christ, as we build, in Christ, the beloved community. We call this process of being changed and growing in love *ecclesial integration/inclusion*. In it, we strengthen the bonds of communion in Christ, which are animated by the Holy Spirit and made manifest in Baptism and the Eucharist. The principle of ecclesial integration/inclusion is particularly important when we seek to strengthen the bonds of communion in Christ among faithful from diverse cultures, races, and ethnicities, and in welcoming new immigrants.

More concretely, the principle of ecclesial integration/inclusion seeks to welcome new immigrants into our parishes and institutions by developing culturally specific ministries that affirm their Gospel-reflecting cultural values and religious traditions. Beyond that, it calls for mutual enrichment through interaction among all cultural groups present in parishes and other Catholic institutions. Ecclesial integration/inclusion is not to be confused with assimilation. A policy of assimilation expects new immigrants to give up their language, culture, values, and traditions, in order to be accepted as parish members. History shows that a policy of assimilation alienates new Catholic immigrants from the Church, thus making them more vulnerable to proselytizing religious groups and to secularization. More than two hundred years of Catholic history in the United States shows that the Church is at its best when it embraces cultural diversity through the principle of ecclesial integration/inclusion—that is, when it takes into account the cultural values, traditions, and faith expressions of new immigrants as an integral part of their being.

Ecclesial Integration/Inclusion in the United States

The principle of ecclesial integration/inclusion was the foundation of the *national parish model*. National parishes were designed as a pastoral response to provide new European Catholic immigrants with the ecclesial space they needed to live their faith, to pray, and to worship in the context of their own culture, language, and traditions. The national parishes were very successful in helping new European immigrants and their children strengthen their Catholic identity while adapting to life in the United States over time. Much of the U.S. Catholic school system stemmed out of the national parishes as a way to make sure that future generations would inherit the Catholic faith.

The success of the *national parish model* in welcoming Catholic immigrants from Europe through a process of ecclesial integration/inclusion is a major reason for having more than seventy million Catholics living in the United States today. The Church's success among African American and Native American Catholics over two centuries has also hinged on the degree to which the Church was able to inculturate gospel values into the very heart of these cultures.

The years following World War II saw the *national parish model* fade away due to the end of massive immigration from Europe. A few years later, the end of segregation and the massive wave of immigrants from the Southern Hemisphere contributed to the cultural diversity we experience today in our neighborhoods and parishes. These historical factors, combined with the limited number of priests and financial resources, are the context in which the shared parish emerges as a pastoral response that gives new life to the Church today.

The principle of ecclesial integration/inclusion that made the *national parish model* so successful is also at the very heart of the *shared parish model*. The difference between the two models is that each national parish served Catholics from a particular European country, normally under the leadership of a priest from that country, and at a time when the Catholic Church was growing significantly, while a shared parish serves people from different cultures and ethnicities, all sharing one pastor, buildings, schedules, and other resources. Often these parishes are put under the leadership of a new immigrant pastor. Such sharing of space and resources can be very challenging at times, but it also makes room for God's grace to fashion the beloved community he calls us to be.

The Scriptural Model for Unity in Diversity

The Scriptures and Christian tradition inspire and guide the Church in understanding and building ecclesial unity amid human diversity. In the Old Testament, Isaiah preaches about God gathering not just Israel but all the nations to his holy mountain in peace (Is 2:2–4). In the New Testament, we hear St. Peter proclaim that "God shows no partiality," as he relates how the Holy Spirit has chosen Gentiles, people from a totally different culture, to be baptized without their needing to embrace Jewish customs (Acts 10). The image of the one body is perhaps the most significant expression of honoring diversity while affirming the unity of the one body in Christ. St. Paul spoke to the Church in Corinth about the diversity of spiritual gifts, and how all of these gifts find their source in the Holy Spirit. Such diversity centers on the actual members of the body, emphasizing their particular cultural identities and/or walk of life. "For in one Spirit we were all baptized into one body, whether Jews or Greeks, slaves or free persons, and we were all given to drink of one Spirit" (1 Cor 12:13). This

UNITY IN DIVERSITY

emphasis to embrace human diversity, particularly in regards to Jews and Greeks, is found throughout the letters of Paul. In the letter to the Galatians, Paul teaches that "there is neither Jew nor Greek, there is neither slave nor free person, there is not male and female; for you are all one in Christ Jesus" (Gal 3:28). A similar statement is found in the letter to the Romans: "For there is no distinction between Jew and Greek; the same Lord is Lord of all, enriching all who call upon him. For 'everyone who calls upon the name of the Lord will be saved'" (Rom 10:12–13). St. Paul requests that Christian leaders "become all things to all" (1 Cor 9:22), and he emphatically argues for a Gospel that does not require Gentiles to become Jews, for in Christ "there is neither Jew nor Greek" (Gal 3:28).

The most famous Christian story about unity in diversity is that of Pentecost in the Acts of the Apostles, sometimes referred to as the "birthday of the Church." In the second chapter of Acts, the Holy Spirit comes down in the form of a driving wind and flames of fire, settling upon the heads of the disciples gathered in the upper room. They immediately begin to announce the Good News of Jesus Christ to the culturally diverse crowd of people gathered nearby for the Jewish feast of Pentecost. All of the Apostles were speaking in their own language of Aramaic, yet each person present heard them in his or her own language. Thus, people retain their own language and culture, yet all are able to share in the Good News.

Chapter 15 in Acts also refers to the equality of Jews and Gentiles in Christ. The statement comes from Peter, but it responds to the inclusivity Paul had preached rendering Jews and Greeks on equal footing before Christ and before God. "My brothers, you are well aware that from early days God made his choice among you that through my mouth the Gentiles would hear the word of the gospel and believe. And God, who knows the heart, bore witness by granting them the holy Spirit just as he did us. He made no distinction between us and them, for by faith he purified their hearts." (Acts 15:7–9)

The example from Acts 6:1–7 is also certainly pertinent as a model of unity in diversity. In this story, the deacons were chosen because the widows of the Hellenists were being neglected. The issue was one of language and therefore nationality and culture, and the goal was inclusion.

The Scriptures and Christian tradition are quite consistent in proclaiming the Gospel to all nations and cultures. They are also clear in presenting a model of ministers capable and willing to "become all things to all." Such a model of ministry is particularly necessary in shared parishes, where pastors may be pulled in different directions by the faithful. The pastor's ministry of unity is paramount in fashioning the beloved community in his parish. All the pastors involved in the consultation agreed that the most important factor for achieving a high degree of ecclesial integration/inclusion in shared parishes is a pastor who has embraced all culturally diverse parishioners as his own. Whether the pastor is U.S.-born or foreign-born, and regardless of what racial/ethnic/cultural group he comes from, the pastor is the primary sign of unity and pastoral love in the parish along with the diocesan bishop. It is quite improbable for a shared parish to achieve a high level of ecclesial integration/inclusion if the pastor does not model such pastoral solicitude for all the parishioners.

The Ministry and Spirituality of the Pastor

The Catholic Church is, at its very heart, a eucharistic community. It is in the celebration of the Sunday Liturgy that Catholics grow ever closer to Christ as his disciples and as members of his Church. Christ left us the gift of himself in the Eucharist, which is actualized in the liturgical ministry of the Apostles and their successors. As the number of the baptized grew over time, the bishops ordained priests as an extension of their apostolic ministry so that every baptized person could share in the Sacrament of the Eucharist and in the entire life and mission of the Church. When a priest is appointed as pastor of a parish by his bishop, that priest becomes responsible for the well-being of all the people living within the parish boundaries. As pastor, the priest becomes a symbol of unity for the faithful entrusted to his care, not only *in persona Christi* during the celebration of the Eucharist, but also as a person who mediates God's love for everyone, regardless of cultural, racial, or ethnic differences. Staff and parish leaders look to their pastor for leadership as they find effective ways for ministering among culturally diverse communities in a spirit of unity in diversity.

The spirituality described by John Paul II in *Ecclesia in America* speaks eloquently about the spirituality that sustains the pastor and his ministry. Such spirituality has a missionary character that constantly seeks an encounter with the living Jesus Christ as the way to conversion, communion, and solidarity. Parish staff and leaders ministering among diverse

SPIRITUALITY FOR ECCLESIAL INTEGRATION/INCLUSION

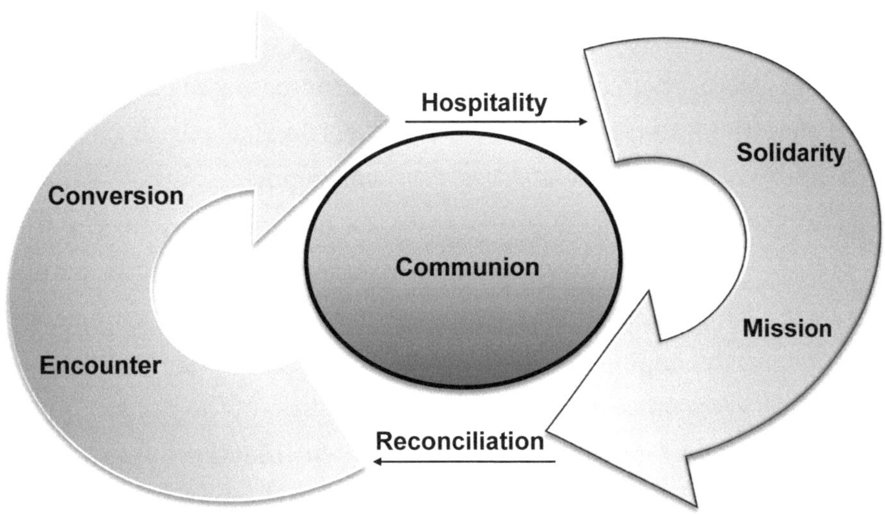

populations are also inspired and moved by the Holy Spirit to create an environment of spiritual intimacy where parishioners from different cultural backgrounds and ethnicities can experience a personal encounter with Christ that leads them to conversion, communion, and solidarity with one another.

The following reflections are based on the comments shared by the pastors participating in the consultation. They apply not only to the pastors themselves but also to their staff and to key leaders in the parish. The consensus of the pastors indicated that the best way to know that you are being effective in bringing people closer to Christ is when you feel closer to Christ when you are interacting with them.

> **Encounter:** Pastors and their teams are ready and capable to relate at a personal level with parishioners from different cultures and backgrounds. Feeling welcomed and comfortable with one another is the key to experiencing God's love, whether in the liturgy, in the classroom, in social events, carrying out works of mercy, in significant family events, or responding to someone who asks for help. We are indeed the voice, the arms, the feet, and the love of Christ when we relate to others as ministers of the Body of Christ.
>
> **Conversion:** Our hearts and minds are constantly changing as we experience God's grace in our lives and share it with others. Celebrating the Sunday Liturgy with a cultural community other than your own, hearing the stories of people different from yourself, enjoying the hospitality of an immigrant family that shares with you from their poverty, visiting people at a hospital or in prison, seeing the generosity of a longtime parishioner toward new immigrant families, witnessing the relentless faith in God's love by those who live in poverty in your parish . . . all these experiences lead pastors and their teams to say, "they did more for me than I did for them."
>
> **Communion:** Many shared parishes experience a sense of community during bicultural or multicultural liturgies that are well planned and celebrated in harmony—at parish picnics and other social events where food, music, art, and service are shared and celebrated by all parishioners and when culturally diverse members of the parish work together, in social services like the St. Vincent de Paul ministry, in lobbying days, painting the church building, gathering for a procession on Good Friday, participating in prayer groups, making decisions as parish council members, managing resources as financial council members, organizing fund-raising activities, serving one another as staff members, and learning together during an in-service on the mission and function of the parish council.
>
> **Solidarity:** Supporting a just and humane immigration reform under the principles of Catholic social

teaching, reaching out to the elderly and the sick, actively supporting ministries serving unwed mothers and broken families, promoting a culture of life and the dignity of the human person from conception to natural death, helping families achieve a higher educational attainment, particularly young people of new immigrant families, and developing a sister parish relationship with another parish in the diocese or in another country are all examples of how solidarity is lived in an intercultural parish.

According to the pastors involved in the consultation, two of the most important spiritual dimensions in shared parishes are hospitality and reconciliation. These two scriptural catalysts of Christian life are like hinges of ministry in shared parishes, and in any family, parish, or Catholic institution for that matter.

Hospitality: In the context of shared parishes, we are called to welcome one another, particularly the stranger among us. Hospitality is not an isolated action or gesture to welcome others. Being hospitable tells the other person "there is room for you." In Scripture, hospitality is a value and a principle; it is a way of being in the world with God and with one another. God is the gracious host. God gathers us around his table. It is Jesus who washes the feet of the

HOSPITALITY

disciples and prepares breakfast for the disciples by the seashore. God models for us a transforming hospitality with a passion for service to others, especially those in most need. In a biblical sense, a hospitable parish is one that knows how to welcome others and does so because that is what the Gospel calls us to do. That is what the Church calls us to do. The great mandate to make disciples of all nations implies welcoming people of all nations so that they will know we are Christian in the way we love one another. The prophet Isaiah speaks of this call to hospitality:

> *I will give them, in my house and within my walls, a monument and a name. Better than sons and daughters; an eternal name, which shall not be cut off, will I give them. . . . For my house shall be called a house of prayer for all peoples.* (Is 56:5–7)

The pastors who participated in the consultation for the elaboration of this guide excel at making people from different cultures and ethnicities feel welcome in God's house. Such an attitude of welcome is also present in their staff and parish leadership, as they see in all the faithful the inheritance God has commended to their care. Dr. Timothy Matovina speaks of "homecoming" as the kind of hospitality parishes need to offer to newcomers. Homecoming welcomes Catholic immigrants not as guests but as full members of the Catholic Church by virtue of their Baptism. In Scripture, mission and hospitality are intertwined. God seeks us and welcomes us all the time as a loving Shepherd. We are called to be the same with one another so every Catholic feels at home.

Just as a welcoming smile can be the beginning of a friendship, a welcoming parish seeks to make people feel at home and develop a sense of belonging to the faith community. A sense of belonging can in turn lead to a sense of ownership, as newcomers embrace fully their call to discipleship as members of a particular parish. It is important to note that a spirituality of hospitality transforms not only those doing the welcoming, but also those being welcomed. Welcoming the stranger means loving the stranger. In a sense, we are all strangers until we get to know one another and relate to one another in God's love for us.

Reconciliation: Along with hospitality, reconciliation is the other hinge that supports the process of ecclesial integration/inclusion. The pastors who participated in the consultation were emphatic about the importance of listening deeply to the concerns often raised by longtime parishioners regarding newcomers. Demographic shifts in towns and neighborhoods can be unsettling for longtime residents used to a certain way of doing things—hearing a certain language, seeing familiar faces, and interacting with people they know. Change is particularly challenging when longtime parishioners from a culturally homogeneous community learn that they need to welcome new Catholic immigrants of different cultural/ethnic background as members of the parish. The prospect of sharing the facilities and resources of the parish with people they don't know can generate a sense of loss of their own space and a fear that the newcomers may not take good care of things, or may even take over the parish that has been such an important part of their lives. Words like *my grandparents built this parish*, or, *it was so difficult for us to finally have a parish we can call our own and now they may take over*, express feelings of uncertainty, loss, and even mourning that are quite real and need to be taken seriously. These experiences often lead many in the receiving community to play the role of a *hesitant host*.

Just as important is the need to be attentive to the struggles and traumatic experiences that may bring newcomers to our towns and neighborhoods. Most immigrants were forced to leave their home and families because of poverty, violence, or persecution, and live in a different country with a different language and culture. For those who are Catholic, in many instances the Catholic Church, particularly the parish, is the one place where they may look for some degree of safety and trust, for a "home away from home." Often times, however, they find structures that may not operate in the familiar ways of the Catholic parishes they used to know back home. They may feel ignored, experience rejection, and even suffer discrimination in their new environment. Often, these experiences also make them feel or act as *reluctant guests*.

Bringing together these two realities of *hesitant host* and *reluctant guest* call for a true ministry of reconciliation that can bridge the gap between well-established parishioners and newcomers. Such a ministry of reconciliation can only be inspired by the Holy Spirit and modeled by Christ. The Scriptures and our Catholic tradition are a living witness to the work of the Spirit, bridging the gap between rich and poor, Jew and Gentile, landlord and stranger. It is up to each generation and each particular parish to continue this ministry of reconciliation as the way to build the beloved community in our shared parishes and in all our Catholic institutions. Listening deeply to the concerns and fears of both the longtime parishioners and the newcomers, and accompanying them as they grieve the loss of what was familiar to them, is at the heart of a ministry of reconciliation in shared parishes.

PART III

The Developmental Process of Ecclesial Integration/Inclusion and Stewardship in Shared Parishes

The Nine Movements for Ecclesial Integration/Inclusion

The third part of this guide focuses on how ecclesial integration/inclusion is actually achieved in shared parishes. The pastors participating in the consultation agreed that ecclesial integration/inclusion is a developmental process that takes place over time and is guided by the unifying love of the Holy Spirit. The pastors affirmed that it follows a process that moves people from *welcoming* to *belonging* to *ownership*. The pastors also emphasized that the higher the level of ecclesial integration/inclusion, the higher the level of stewardship in shared parishes.

The benchmarks of *welcoming, belonging,* and *ownership* resonate with Fr. Robert Schreiter's goals for ministry in multicultural settings. *Welcoming* relates to the goal of *recognition of the other as different.* It involves acknowledging their presence and showing hospitality in a way the other understands. *Belonging* relates to the goal of *respecting cultural differences* and describes how relationships across cultural boundaries take shape. *Ownership* relates to the goal of *healthy interaction,* described as a kind of communion in which neither group loses its own identity but has taken to itself elements of the other group. There is a sense of joint ownership and trust that allows for generous interaction with one another. The developmental aspect of this process is also based on a common sense approach: welcoming leads to a sense of belonging, which in turn leads to a

FROM NEWCOMERS TO STEWARDS OF THE FAITH COMMUNITY

sense of ownership and healthier intercultural relationships.

In order to provide a roadmap for achieving the benchmarks of *welcome, belonging,* and *ownership,* this guide presents nine movements or indicators that describe how ecclesial integration/inclusion is actually achieved. It is important to note that the nine movements don't describe a program or a rigid method. Rather, the nine movements illustrate a dynamic human process of *welcome, belonging,* and *ownership* that involves the pastoral accompaniment of the faithful by the pastor and his team. This pastoral process echoes the words expressed by Pope Francis during his first homily as Pope:

> My wish is that all of us, after these days of grace, will have the courage, yes, the courage, to walk in the presence of the Lord, with the Lord's Cross; to build the Church on the Lord's blood, which was poured out on the Cross; and to profess the one glory: Christ crucified. And in this way, the Church will go forward. (Pope Francis, Homily, March 14, 2013)

The dynamic process of ecclesial integration/inclusion calls us to the ongoing process of walking with the faithful entrusted to our care, building the beloved community among them, and professing Christ's Death and Resurrection as the primary reason for our hope and our mission.

The following example unfolds the nine movements for ecclesial integration/inclusion in the context of a shared parish. The example presents a parish where a significant number of Vietnamese and Hispanic families have recently arrived. The threefold goal of the pastor and his team is to achieve a high

PROCESS FOR ECCLESIAL INTEGRATION/INCLUSION

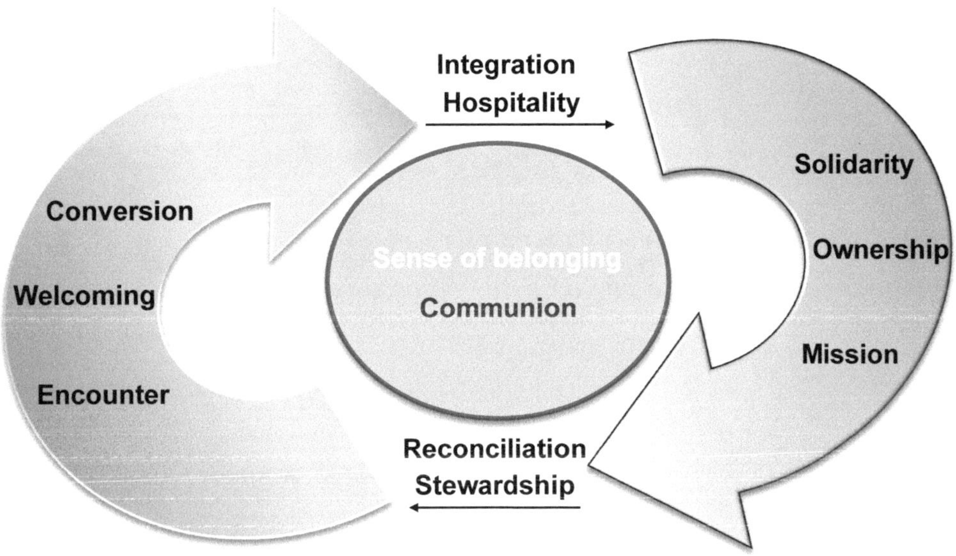

level of *welcoming, belonging,* and *ownership* among the culturally diverse Catholic groups living within the parish boundaries. Besides working as a roadmap, the benchmarks can also be used to assess the level of stewardship among new immigrants, which grows in direct proportion to the level of ecclesial integration/inclusion achieved.

The example uses the basic structure present in many parishes—pastor, staff, parish council, and financial council—to illustrate how this structure shifts as the process of ecclesial integration/inclusion moves forward. It highlights the kind of leadership style most needed from the pastor to move the process forward. The example also includes three moments of crisis often faced in shared parishes. The first crisis has to do with the resistance to change, the second with the resistance to sharing, and the third with the resistance to mutual ownership.

Welcoming

Movement 1: Mission

After becoming aware of the significant presence of Vietnamese and Hispanic Catholics living within the parish boundaries, the pastor makes the decision to reach out to them. A group of parish leaders is organized to conduct a census in areas where a significant number of new Vietnamese and Hispanic immigrants live. The census is conducted in a spirit of mission, bringing greetings from the pastor to those visited, along with an invitation to take part in the life and mission of the parish as their home. The pastor's leadership style in the first movement is proactive, with an emphasis on the mission to reach out to all peoples residing within the parish boundaries.

MOVEMENT 1—MISSION

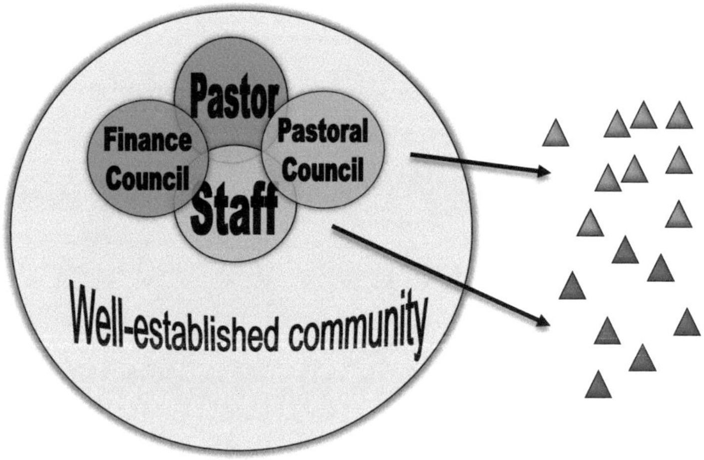

Parish Territory

Movement 2: Homecoming

A few Vietnamese and Hispanic families respond to the invitation of the pastor right away and begin attending the Sunday Liturgy in English. However, the vast majority do not feel comfortable taking part in the Mass or other parish activities in English and with people they do not know. Realizing the importance of language, culture, and religious traditions of new Catholic immigrants, the pastor decides to create an *ecclesial space* for Vietnamese and Hispanics in his parish by providing culturally specific ministries for these new communities. Creating an *ecclesial space* begins by establishing the Sunday Liturgy in Vietnamese and Spanish. Such a decision is the sign *par excellence* that Vietnamese and Hispanics, in this case, have been welcomed not only as individuals but also as communities with specific needs and aspirations as baptized Catholics. The decision made by the pastor to establish the Mass in a language other than English often leads to a *crisis*. Staff and other parish leaders may be concerned about the implications this change may have. It is common to think that having the Mass offered in different languages will divide the parish. However, the pastor knows that the parish is already divided between those baptized Catholics who are already gathered and those who are scattered.

The experience in more than seven thousand parishes across the United States shows that offering the Sunday Liturgy in the language and cultural context of new Catholic immigrants creates the initial conditions for interaction and unity. It provides new immigrants with the ecclesial space they need to strengthen their Catholic identity and adapt to life in the United States from a position of strength. It also gives them the opportunity to develop a ministerial capacity, beginning with liturgical ministries and the formation of a leadership team to coordinate ministries. The establishment of the Sunday Liturgy in Vietnamese or Spanish often requires the assistance of priests who can celebrate the Mass in those languages while the pastor develops

MOVEMENT 2—HOMECOMING: MAKE PEOPLE FEEL AT HOME

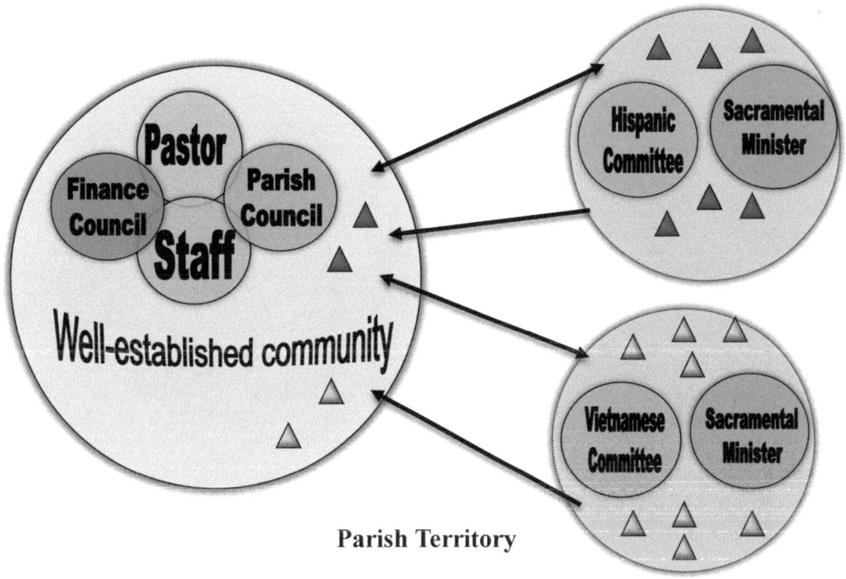

the skill of doing so himself. However, *ecclesial clarity* is of essence in recognizing that the pastoral responsibility for all parishioners belongs to the pastor. A clear understanding on the part of the sacramental minister that he is assisting the pastor in his ministry, not taking over as "*de facto* pastor" of the Vietnamese or the Hispanic community, has proven to be extremely helpful in avoiding confusion and potential conflict. Establishing the Sunday Liturgy in Vietnamese and Spanish is a necessary step toward achieving unity in diversity in the future. The practice of stewardship takes place in the form of time and talent offered by newcomers, particularly within their respective communities. The sharing of treasure is often quite limited at this point.

Movement 3: Ministerial Growth

Once the Sunday Liturgy is in place, both the Vietnamese and the Hispanic communities begin to develop ministries and ministers. First, liturgical ministries are developed, then catechetical formation for the reception of the sacraments takes place. Other ministries follow in the area of prayer, social services, youth ministry, community building, stewardship, and others. In some cases, particularly with the Latino community, this process is aided by the establishment and strong presence of lay ecclesial movements and small ecclesial communities. The successful development of ministries leads to the growing size and participation of the new communities and to their need for more resources.

This growth results in a *second crisis* that calls for a change in the way resources are used, which is often expressed through complaining. On the one hand, the newcomers develop a sense of belonging to the parish that enables them to expect more resources on the way, such as a better schedule for their Sunday Liturgy, the use of the new hall, a catechetical program that allows parents to teach the faith to their own children, the celebration of traditions particular to their culture,

MOVEMENT 3—MINISTERIAL GROWTH: ORGANIZE AND DEVELOP MINISTRIES AND MINISTERS

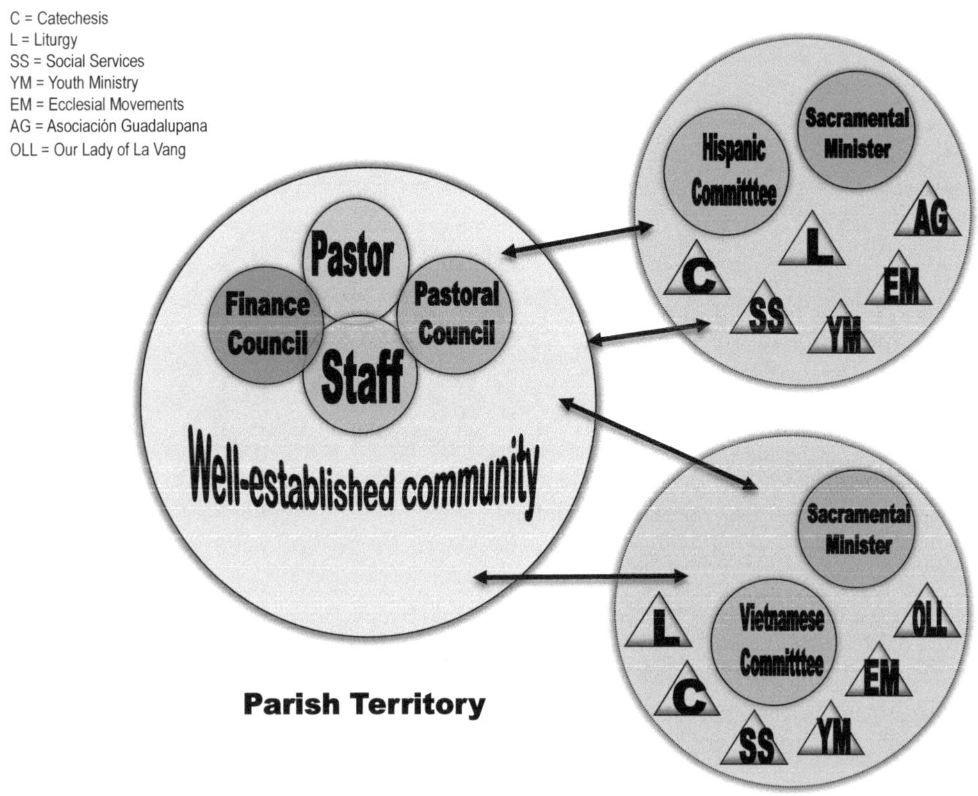

and so forth. On the other hand, longtime parishioners begin to complain about the constant demand of the newcomers for more access in terms of time, space, and programs, or that the pastors spend too much time with them. Hearing people's complaints is not very pleasant. However, it is a sign of the leadership's success, because it shows that the newcomers have developed a sense of belonging to the parish. It also signals the need to focus on building relationships across cultures so people can move from "us–them" language to "we" language.

It is not unusual for shared parishes to get stuck in this movement as people from the various communities work hard at "tolerating" each other and avoiding conflict. This kind of tolerance of the other is not enough to continue on the path toward a healthy interaction between the culturally diverse members of the parish. Only when people are willing to develop relationships across cultures and ministries can the parish community, as a whole, advance on the path toward ecclesial integration/inclusion. The pastor's leadership style at this point warrants very good listening skills and creates an environment of safety and trust where the leaders of the different communities can share their concerns and begin a process of intercultural dialogue and mutual understanding. The level of stewardship increases significantly in terms of time and talent. Treasure can also be significant, depending on the freedom the Vietnamese and Hispanic communities have to develop ministries and ministers and to practice forms of fund raising relevant to each community. The offering during Mass may still be limited since practices such as using the envelope or committing to giving a fixed weekly amount may be foreign to them.

Belonging

Movement 4: Building Relationships Across Cultures

This movement is perhaps the most difficult to achieve. One of the reasons is that it requires leaders from the culturally different communities to go beyond their cultural boundaries in order to meet and get to know one another on a more personal level. Sharing stories and perspectives and having common experiences lead to the development of interpersonal relationships that move people from "us–them" language to "we" language. The celebration of multicultural liturgies on key feast days, annual picnics where the entire community comes together for fun and food, annual festivals planned and implemented with involvement from different groups and organizations, and retreats focusing on sharing and listening to one another's stories in the context of the Scriptures, among others, are all effective ways for building relationships and a greater sense of community.

There was consensus among the pastors participating in the consultation that the

MOVEMENT 4—BUILD RELATIONSHIPS ACROSS CULTURES AND MINISTRIES

pastor's love for parishioners of all cultural groups is one of the most, if not the most, important indicators that a shared parish has reached the fourth movement on the process of ecclesial integration/inclusion. Such pastoral love is reflected in the fact that the pastor knows the leadership of the different cultural communities on a personal level, and he is actively and regularly present at the liturgical and social celebrations of the different cultural communities. The pastor is trusted by all the faithful and models unity in diversity to his staff and leaders, thus becoming a symbol of unity for all. At this stage of the integration process, the visiting sacramental minister is usually no longer needed, as the pastor and/or a parish vicar are able to preside at the Sunday Liturgies in English, Vietnamese, and Spanish. (Pastoral realities, however, may dictate otherwise.) Time and talent continue to grow at a fast rate as the communities expand. The question of the weekly contribution may come up as an issue as the various communities in the parish get to know each other more. This movement also presents a good opportunity for exploring creative ways of fund raising.

Movement 5: Intercultural Leadership Development and Formation

This movement emphasizes the need to mentor and form parish leaders to be interculturally competent. Members of the parish and financial councils and parish staff are aware of the cultural differences present in the parish and know how to communicate, work, and relate across cultural boundaries. There is a commitment to the ongoing development of intercultural competency in the form of attitudes, knowledge, and skills that better serve a culturally diverse parish. The ongoing development of intercultural competence requires financial support for staff and parish leaders to participate in trainings, in-services, classes, and workshops that help leaders achieve a high level of intercultural competency. The overall ministerial development of leaders from the Vietnamese and Hispanic community is also essential in order for them to be hireable as parish staff in the future. The pastor is a mentor and a coach to the emerging leadership within the various communities as they become more interculturally competent. Stewardship becomes a subject of study and skill development, as the diverse cultural/ethnic communities learn from one another and collaborate more closely. It also prepares the parish leadership to be more inclusive in the decision-making process.

Movement 6: Decision-Making Process

This movement triggers the *third* common *crisis*: going from the dynamic *hosts-guests* to a common sense of ownership. A shared parish that has reached this level of ecclesial integration/inclusion shows members of the different cultural communities as having a place at the table where decisions are made, such as the parish council, the finance council, and even the staff. The movement highlights the desire of leaders from the Vietnamese and Hispanic communities to work for the well-being of the entire parish, not only members of their particular cultural group. At the same time, the leadership of the

MOVEMENT 5—CHAMPION LEADERSHIP DEVELOPMENT AND FORMATION

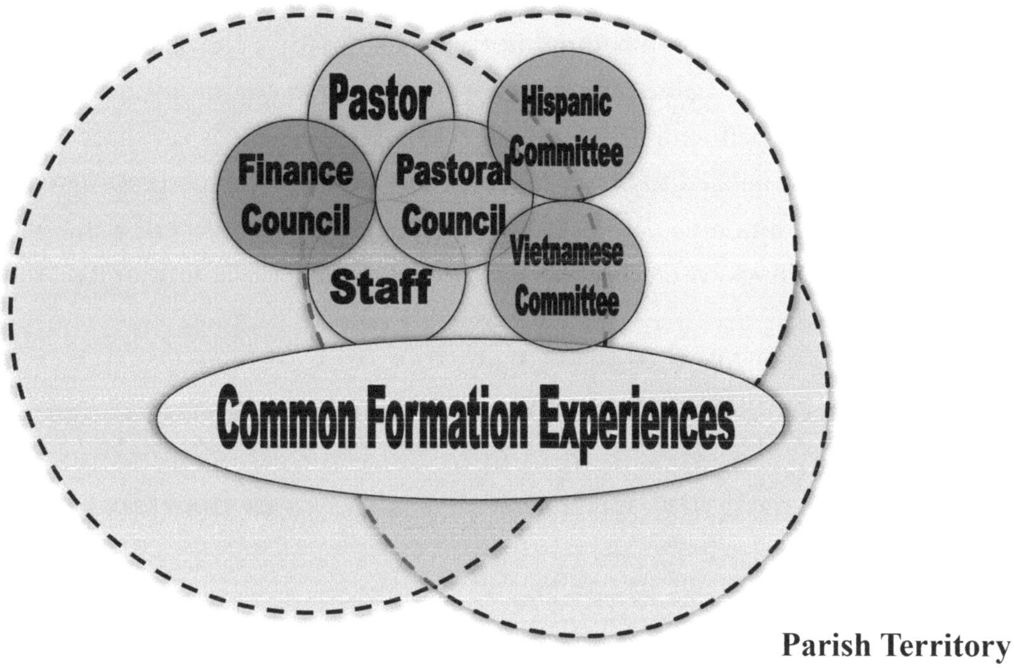

MOVEMENT 6—OPEN WIDE THE DOORS TO THE DECISION-MAKING PROCESS

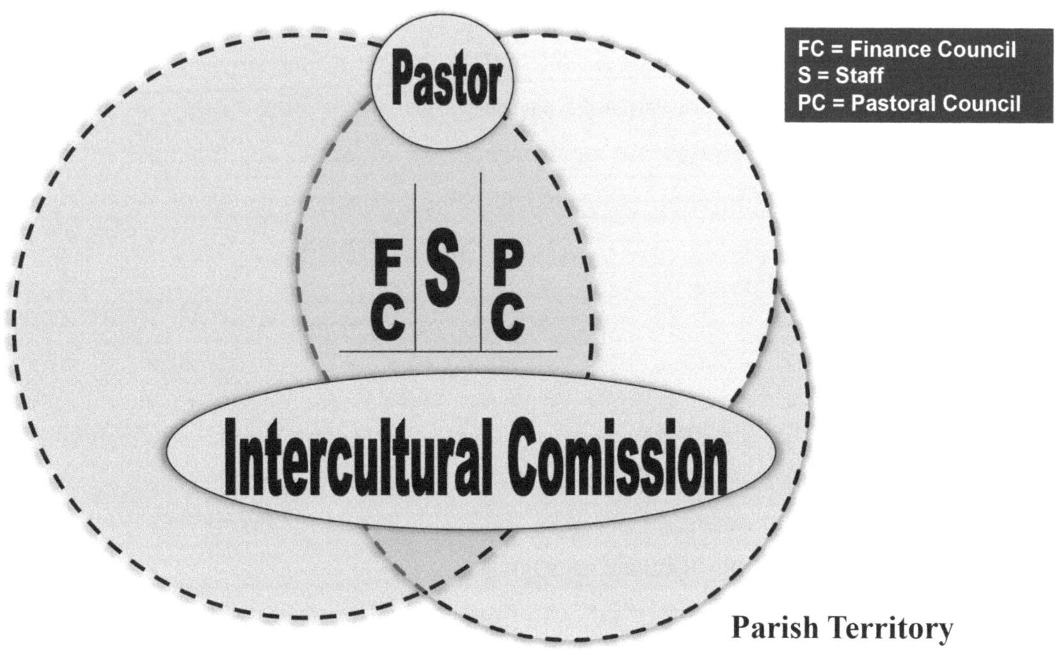

longstanding community is ready to embrace the new leaders as cohosts and as partners on equal footing.

At this point of development, the structure and leadership of the parish community is representative of the culturally diverse members and is equipped with the attitudes, knowledge, and skills needed to better serve the entire parish community. The principle of "having to do things yourself, but not alone" applies to staff that may not have a particular language skill, like Vietnamese, but know how to involve leaders from the Vietnamese community to work with them in order to accomplish the desired outcomes of a particular program or activity. The pastor's leadership emphasizes his role as a facilitator who knows how to encourage a high level of participation and collaboration, and how to handle difficult situations through prayerful discernment. There is a significant development in the sharing of treasure on the part of the Vietnamese and Hispanic communities since they are included in the decision-making process of the parish as a whole. Leaders from these two communities are no longer concerned only with the well-being of their particular community.

Ownership

Movement 7: Sharing Resources

A sense of ownership is achieved with this movement as a direct result of an inclusive decision-making process. Shared parishes achieving this level of ecclesial integration present a culturally diverse leadership directly involved in the development of the parish budget. Decisions on the use of facilities, the scheduling of activities (including Masses in different languages), and the selection of particular programs take into consideration the needs and aspirations of the diverse communities present in the parish. It is very likely for shared parishes at this level of ecclesial integration to have mission statements that describe the parish as a culturally diverse community. The following are some examples:

> *"We are a multicultural and diverse community united by our faith in God."*
>
> (St. Philip Benizi, Jonesboro, GA)

> *"We believe that the various cultures within our community are gifts from God, and rather than assimilate them, we seek to be enriched by them."*
>
> (St. Francis de Sales, Holland, MI)

> *"Bring all people, all races, all ethnic groups, into full union with Christ."*
>
> (Our Lady of Lourdes, Montclair, CA)

> *"Multicultural community that strives to proclaim the Gospel in our neighborhoods and beyond."*
>
> (St. Camillus, Silver Spring, MD)

> *"Accepting God's gifts of love calls us to share our gifts with others, including the poor, the refugees, the immigrants."*
>
> (St. Joseph's Parish, Amarillo, TX)

The pastor's leadership style provides strategic thinking, good administration of spiritual, human, and material resources,

MOVEMENT 7—SHARING RESOURCES: STRENGTHEN A SENSE OF OWNERSHIP

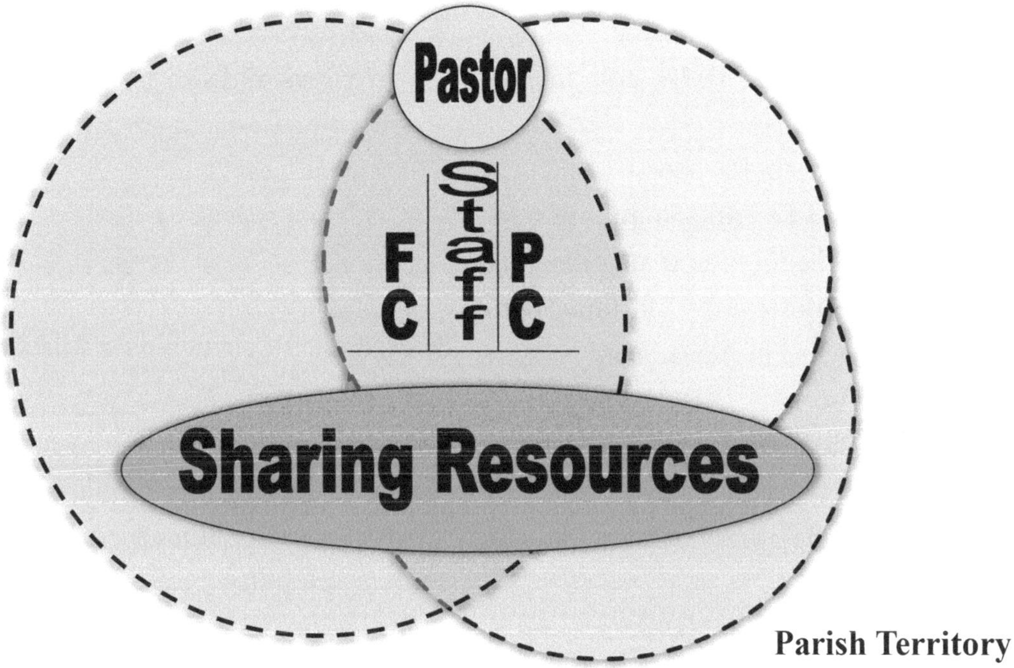

and guidance for the leadership to achieve a clear vision and mission for the parish as a whole. The leaders of the different cultural communities know the overall resources and needs of the entire parish and sit at the table where decisions are made regarding the use of all resources. They know how the different cultural communities benefit and how the overall mission of the parish is fulfilled.

This results in a significantly more generous share of their treasure, and all are more receptive to the practice of increasing and regularizing their weekly offering.

Movement 8: Achieving Stewardship

The high level of ownership leads to a generous and responsible sharing of time, talent, and treasure on the part of all ethnic/cultural communities engaged in the life and mission of the shared parish. There is an appreciation of the different styles and means by which the different ethnic/cultural communities contribute to the life of and do fund raising for the parish. Collaboration is quite high across cultures, ministries, and activities, and personal relationships are strong among the members of the finance council, parish council, and staff. The pastor's role is more supportive in this movement since the vision, structure, and leadership of the parish are in place and working well. Pastors consulted for the elaboration for this guide identified the following ideas as helpful for achieving a high level of stewardship in shared parishes:

- Allow the communities of a parish to be different communities together
- Develop close relationships with key leaders from each ethnic community
- Be open to different styles and means of stewardship
- Plan with people, not for people
- Find ways for different communities to support each other in their struggles
- Emphasize the positive by affirming people already engaged in stewardship
- Acknowledge need
- Explain simply and regularly how resources are used
- Avoid comparing one cultural group to another
- Avoid either/or thinking by embracing a both/and mentality
- Find ways for people to symbolize and ritualize their stewardship
- Come up with a catchphrase all can recite
- Develop and empower leadership instead of doing things for them
- Find ways for people to contribute their hard work and sweat
- Bury the dead and pay attention to grief
- Dine with everyone
- Celebrate successes

Movement 9: Communion in Mission

This movement is less a point of arrival than a new beginning in the mission of the Church to bring the Good News of Jesus Christ to every human situation. Growing human mobility and ongoing population shifts require that our parishes be welcoming communities of disciples in a constant state of mission. The movement also clarifies that the goal of shared parishes is to bring the

MOVEMENT 8—SOW AND REAP FULL OWNERSHIP AND STEWARDSHIP

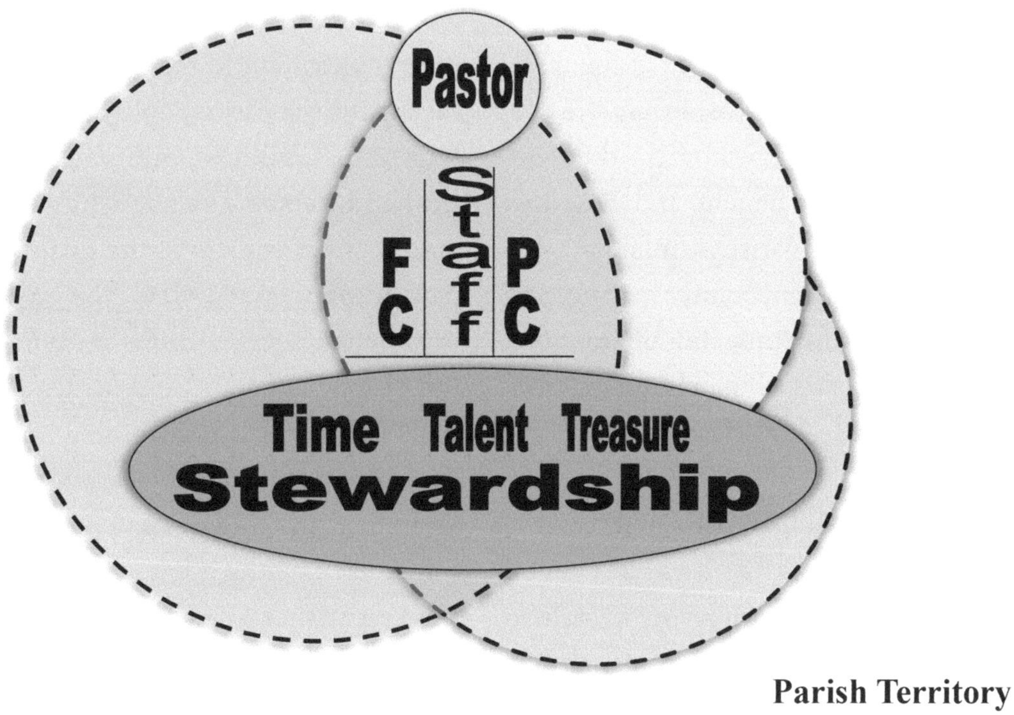

culturally diverse members of the parish to a high level of ecclesial integration/inclusion with one another as members of the one Body of Christ. The point of reference is the Gospel, lived out as disciples of Christ and with the guidance of the Holy Spirit. All cultures in the shared parish are transformed in Christ and brought together in a more perfect union with one another and with God.

The following values and practices from Scripture were identified by the pastors as examples of what ministry should look like in shared parishes:

- Gn 18:2–8: Abraham and Sarah's reception of the three mysterious strangers at the oak of Mamre.
- Gn 22:17: "I will bless you and make your descendants as countless as the stars of the sky and the sands of the seashore."
- Lv 19:33–34: "When an alien resides with you in your land . . ."
- Ruth: The entire book as it reflects upon salvation through a foreigner.
- Sir 2:5: "In fire gold is tested."
- Is 55:1–11: "All you who are thirsty, come to the water . . ."
- Mt 8:20: "The Son of Man has nowhere to rest his head."
- Mt 25:35: "I was . . . a stranger and you welcomed me."
- Acts 2:12: "What does this mean?"
- Acts 6:1–7: "Brothers, select from among you seven reputable men, filled with the Spirit and wisdom, whom we shall appoint to this task . . ."
- Rom 8:31b–39: "If God is for us, who can be against us?"
- 1 Cor 12:12–22: "As a body is one though it has many parts . . ."

MOVEMENT 9—ACHIEVE FULL COMMITMENT TO THE MISSION OF THE PARISH

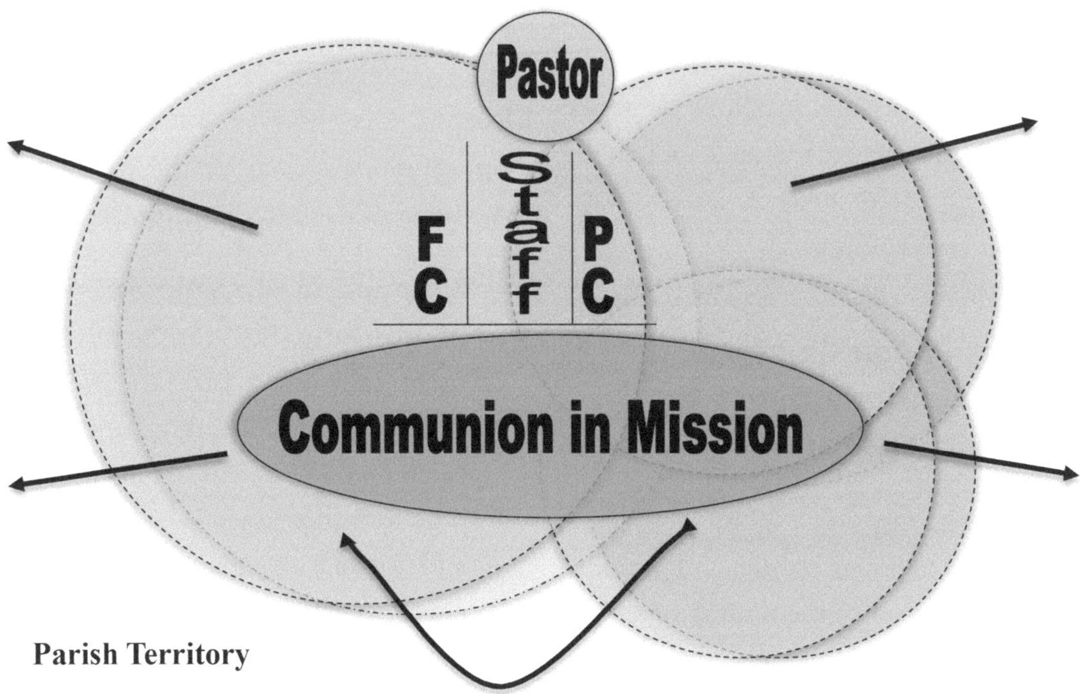

QUESTIONS FOR REFLECTION

1) In which of the nine movements do you place your shared parish at this point of its development?
2) What actions have helped move this development forward?
3) What is getting in the way of further development?
4) What are some pastoral actions you can take at this point to overcome the obstacles?
5) To what degree are the pastor and his team on the same page regarding the goals and process to achieve ecclesial integration/inclusion?
6) What can facilitate a conversation between the pastor and his team to bring intercultural relationships and collaboration to a higher level?

- Gal 3:27–29: "For all of you who were baptized into Christ have clothed yourselves with Christ. There is neither Jew nor Greek . . ."
- Rev 7:9–10: "from every nation, race, people, and tongue. They stood before the throne . . ."

In the box above are questions for reflection as you ponder the roadmap for achieving ecclesial integration/inclusion and stewardship in your own community.

A Shared Parish Illustration of the Nine Movements for Ecclesial Integration/Inclusion

The following responses come from St. Joseph's Parish in Amarillo, Texas. They illustrate the application of the nine movements in the parish's particular context. In addition to the nine movements, the responses illustrate how the parish has managed conflict and achieved healing in particular situations. The experiences are included in the guide to generate ideas for possible pastoral action in shared parishes around the country. Similar experiences are found in the other parishes that participated in the consultation. St. Joseph's was chosen for the rich variety of communities served by the parish and the creativity of its pastoral responses.

a) **Meet people where they are in a spirit of mission:** The parish mission statement calls the parish to "welcome all God's children." Weekly Sunday Mass is celebrated in English, Spanish, and Dinka. One monthly Mass is bilingual (English and Dinka), and the majority of the catechists, kindergarten through high school, are bilingual (English and Spanish). The

Sudanese community provides their own bilingual catechists (English and Dinka).

b) **Practice hospitality:** Every three months, the parish leadership hosts a welcome dinner for all new parishioners. Coffee and donuts or *pan dulce* (sweet bread) are offered after all Sunday Masses on the first weekend of the month. The weekly bulletin has a Spanish-language section, and everything that is printed in the bulletin is in both languages even if the information pertains to only one language group. The staff is bilingual. Announcements in Mass are done in English, Spanish, and Dinka in common liturgical celebration, and the pastor is bilingual—English and Spanish—and is learning Dinka.

c) **Provide culturally specific ministries:** *In liturgy and prayer life*: All liturgical celebrations are available in all three primary languages—English, Spanish, and Dinka. Each language group has liturgical ministers who speak their language and those who can lead the congregation in other non-sacramental liturgical or devotional celebrations in their native language, e.g. Rosaries, wake services, novenas, Stations of the Cross, etc.

In faith formation and leadership development: Adult faith formation is offered in each of the three primary languages with native leaders. Each group has their own faith formation program that reflects their reality and level of catechesis. The parish is in the process of selecting candidates for the permanent diaconate that reflect each of the three language groups.

In social services and social justice ministries: Any need of services for one group is communicated to the others groups. For example, during the Thanksgiving and Christmas holidays families from each of the language groups that are in need are sponsored by another family or parish organization that does not necessarily come from the same language group. Parishioners have offered money for funerals of the poor in the community and have "adopted" children of poor families to provide clothing during the winter months. ESL classes are offered in the parish.

In building community across cultures and ministries: The parish provides multicultural and trilingual celebrations for all major feast days and cultural celebrations; a trilingual choir provides all the liturgical music for the Holy Triduum and Christmas celebrations. Catechesis is provided at all cultural religious events to explain to the non-native participants the significance of the particular celebration (e.g., *Dia de los Muertos, Acostamiento del Niño,* Thanksgiving, Our Lady of Guadalupe, Memorial Day, etc.). The parish is working toward integrating the three communities by intentionally hosting the other groups at native celebrations. For example, they have one *Posada* every year that is celebrated in English; the Sudanese community performs their native religious dances to honor Our Lady of Guadalupe; and the Thanksgiving Mass is in English and Spanish.

d) **Foster a Catholic identity across cultures and ministries:** All three language groups are participating in the *Why Catholic?* program by Renew in their own language. The organizing committee has representation from all three communities to maintain a sense of unity. There is an emphasis on the fact that all are going through the same program that unites them as one Catholic Church.

e) **Handle complaining, miscommunication, mistrust, and competition among communities:** Most of these situations are discussed openly at the pastoral council meeting. If it is a sensitive situation, then it is addressed directly by the pastor with input from the persons/groups involved.

f) **Foster a sense of belonging to the parish among its culturally diverse communities:** Representatives/leaders from the three major language groups have keys to the Church and meeting rooms, which reflects the fact that all of them belong and have access to the church and meeting space. They are asked to call in to the office to schedule their events. Everyone has equal opportunity to use the meeting space.

g) **Share stories, common projects, and programs:** In the beginning, the English-speaking community went through an extensive planning process that led to writing a mission statement and setting pastoral goals for the community. The mission statement states: "We are a family united in our Catholic faith that welcomes all God's children to continue the ministry of Christ to love, serve and educate." This mission prepared the community to begin to receive the other groups that God sent to the parish.

Since this mission statement was written, the parish has opened its arms to a Mass in Spanish and to a Mass in Dinka. New infants have also been welcomed into the Church through the Sacrament of Baptism in English, Spanish, Dinka, Croatian, and Creole. Annually, they have a unity Mass that gives the leadership an opportunity to recommit to the original covenant that was written, along with the mission statement that calls them to "unity in Christ." At this Mass, the diocesan bishop presides. The Mass is celebrated in English and Spanish; the Gospel is proclaimed by the pastor in Dinka; one choir sings in all three languages; and the petitions are said in Spanish, Dinka, Croatian, and Tagalog, with each native speaker repeating the petition in English. After the Mass, a community feast takes place that includes all the different cultural groups.

The parish and its parochial school are working on establishing a cultural and language institute for the parishioners. For eleven weeks each summer, language classes will be provided: ESL, Spanish, and Dinka. These classes will be provided simultaneously—in the same building and with breaks taken together. Three to four classes will be provided to all the participants on ecclesial integration based on the bishops' pastoral letter "One Church, Many Cultures."

On Pentecost they have an annual celebration of the multicultural reality of the parish with a trilingual choir (English, Spanish, Dinka). The petitions are offered in these three main languages plus Croatian, Tagalog, and sometimes in Gaelic. The Gospel is proclaimed in English, Spanish, Dinka, and Tagalog. At the end, every reader together with the deacon says, "The Gospel of the Lord."

May Crowning is done every weekend in the month of May. Each language community has the opportunity to crown Mary on a given weekend. All of them follow the same format: representatives from the community join the presider in the entrance procession; a Marian hymn is sung in their native language for the entrance hymn; once they arrive in the sanctuary the singing finishes and someone selected from the community crowns Mary (sometimes a child, other times an elderly lady or a couple); the community leads the congregation in reciting the Hail Mary in their native language; and the presider continues with the Opening Prayer for the Sunday Liturgy. The various communities that participate in the crowning of Mary are English-speaking (of European American and Mexican American descent), Hispanic, Sudanese, Bosnian, Filipino, and Irish.

h) **Invest in the faith formation and leadership development of its leaders and staff:** A fund has been established that helps representatives from the community receive leadership development and training. Since it was just recently established, the focus has been on training individuals in specific ministries that are needed. They have had parishioners trained in youth ministry focusing on "mainstream" teens and also in ministering among Latino/Hispanic immigrant teens through the Fe y Vida Institute. Other adults were trained in faith formation of children using bilingual books. Representatives from the English- and Spanish-speaking communities were sent to the International Catholic Stewardship Conference to begin a stewardship catechetical program in the parish.

i) **Include culturally diverse representation in the parish's decision-making bodies:** The pastoral council has representation from the main English-speaking groups of the parish (four European Americans; six Mexican Americans), as well as two Mexican immigrants and two Sudanese persons. The finance council is made up of one European American, three Mexican Americans, and two Mexican immigrants. The Sudanese community has their own leadership committee, elected by the Sudanese community. The Sudanese community catechists meet with the pastor on a regular basis.

j) **Foster a sense of ownership and stewardship among all parishioners:** All parishioners in their respective languages are invited and encouraged to participate in all aspects of the parish including the maintenance of the buildings and the use of offering envelopes. The pastor is consistent in welcoming all the parishioners in all these aspects of the parish. He also has set up a stewardship committee (after receiving training at the International Catholic Stewardship Conference) to begin to address this area with all the parishioners.

k) **Facilitate decision-making processes:** All groups are consulted in the parish pastoral council. The leadership of all the groups of the parish participates in the meetings to facilitate communications to and from each of the entities.

l) **Facilitate problem solving and conflict resolution between diverse persons and communities:** The parish has become more intentional about ecclesial integration. A process of parish assemblies with the participation of the various communities/families or groups in the parish has begun. The first assembly included a reflection from each group on how they are living the parish mission statement: "We are a Catholic Faith Community that welcomes all God's children to continue the mission of Christ, to love, serve, and educate." The parish logo is "unity in Christ." After each group reflected on how they are living the parish mission statement they each reported back to the entire parish assembly. The discussion and report included their vision for themselves within the stated Mission Statement.

The various groups consisted of lifetime parishioners (older parishioners), the Altar Society, catechists, the youth ministry team, teen leaders, *Pastoral Juvenil Hispana*, school leaders, day care leaders, the RCIA team, the Spanish-speaking community leadership, the finance council, the Sudanese community leadership, etc. A religious sister led with a spiritual reflection on "being Church" and the assembly ended with a ritual of commitment to "unity in Christ." After a short prayer service, one representative from each group came up and placed one hand on the Unity Stone as a sign of their commitment to their mission statement and to unity. At the planned second parish assembly, each group will address the assembly about where they see themselves in the community, what has helped them in the process of integration, and what they still need from each other. The process will consist of a formal request, formal response, and an agreement (covenant) to each other. All of this will be done in a spirit of reflective prayer and celebration.

m) **Handle grief and facilitate healing:** (i.e., the well-established host community feeling that they are losing their parish, and the newcomers and guests dealing with the grief of leaving behind their country and family.)

The pastor has met with various groups separately, to listen to their concerns about the changes in the parish. Numerous meetings with parishioners on a one-to-one basis have also taken place. These have included meeting with some of the long-time European American and Mexican American parishioners that are uncomfortable with the pastor accommodating the newcomers, and also listening to the Sudanese refugees tell their stories and the needs they have from the parish. All of this has been done on an informal basis, as needed, and not necessarily planned.

QUESTIONS FOR REFLECTION

1) Which of these ideas have you implemented in your shared parish?
2) What ideas do you find helpful to further the process of ecclesial integration/inclusion in your shared parish?
3) What will it take to implement them?

Questions for reflection and action on the experience of St. Joseph's Parish are in the box above.

Pastoral Situations and Best Practices in Shared Parishes

The final component of the guide presents pastoral situations that have challenged pastors and their teams. It describes how they have responded to them to achieve a positive outcome. In this sense, the following pastoral responses each exemplify certain best practices. Each pastoral situation includes the following elements to help unpack the pastoral wisdom and process used so that it may be replicated in future pastoral applications in shared parishes:

a) Brief description of the pastoral situation
b) Identification of roles
c) Intercultural competencies utilized: knowledge, attitudes, and skills
d) Insight for pastoral planning
e) Pastoral principle

Pastors and their teams can use this process as a tool to assess a pastoral situation in their particular parish and look for key elements to achieve positive results. The pastoral situations were identified by pastors participating in the consultation and by national leaders of different ethnic/cultural Catholic communities ministering in shared parishes in the United States.

First Pastoral Situation: "Mission and Welcome"

Brief Description of the Pastoral Situation

The pastoral situation takes place in Grand Rapids, Michigan, where a community from Guatemala that spoke Mam (a Mayan dialect) gathered for prayer at a home. The family providing the home came from an agricultural background and had a cornfield in its backyard. The leaders of the Mayan community invited the deacon of the parish to visit them, and he developed a relationship with the community. The deacon in turn invited the pastor. Within a few months the prayer group had grown so that they had to add a wing to the house to accommodate the growing congregation. Eventually, the parish extended an invitation to use the auditorium, but it took two years for the community to accept the invitation. Within a few years the group grew into two separate groups of one hundred people each. The parish eventually purchased a larger church to accommodate the growing Guatemalan community.

Identification of Roles

A Catholic family decides to host a group of Mayan Catholics who want to gather for prayer. They become a bridge to the local parish, and the deacon is invited to meet the groups. The deacon accepts and invites the pastor, aware that he is the decision maker. The pastor asks the parish social committee to be available to the emerging Mayan community. Later on, the pastor consults with the parish council before making the decision to invite the Mayan community to be a part of the parish in a spirit of homecoming.

This pastoral experience describes a missionary action of visiting and welcoming based on Matthew 25. This allows the deacon and the pastor to listen to the story of the Catholic Mayan community living within the parish boundaries. This pastoral response became a ministry of the parish, coordinated with sensitivity, both cultural and social. As the Mayan community experienced being welcomed, they were willing to learn about the parish and began to feel a sense of connection and belonging.

Intercultural Competencies Utilized

Knowledge: Those involved on the receiving side of the community know of the parish responsibility to care for all the people living within the parish boundaries. The host family, the pastor, and the deacon learn about the situation of the Mayan community. The pastor uses the structures and processes in place at the parish to decide on welcoming the Mayan community to share in the life and mission of the parish in a spirit of homecoming.

Skills: The power of persuasion—both on the part of the deacon who brought the situation to the attention of the pastor and on the part of the pastor who brought a response back to the Mayan community and to the larger community. Supervision.

Attitudes: Openness to new possibilities. Risk taking. Moving beyond comfort zones. Generosity, hospitality, and solidarity showed by all people involved.

Pastoral Planning Insight

Need is identified through listening and observing with pastoral sensitivity; through consultation with the pastoral team and decision-making bodies; through overseeing development of ministry; through placement of ministry in the parish context, analysis of resources and allocation, and supervision; and through team work.

Pastoral Principle

Meet people where they are at in a spirit of mission.

Second Pastoral Situation: "Two Parishes Sharing the Same Pastor"

Brief Description of the Pastoral Situation

The pastoral situation involves two predominantly black Catholic parishes within five miles of each other. They shared a common history and heritage but had never come together to do things in common. One parish is predominantly of Creole origin and the other of African American background. Due to a priest shortage in the diocese, the two parishes were asked to share one pastor. The pastor from the Creole parish was assigned to the African American parish, while the pastor from the African American parish was assigned to a parish somewhere else in the diocese. Parishioners from the Creole parish were comfortable with the move since they would keep the same pastor. But parishioners from the African American parish rejected the whole idea of sharing a priest with the other parish.

The pastor assigned to both parishes saw the tension building due to the new arrangement and decided to form a ten-member reconciliation team with representatives of the two parishes to help him navigate the difficult waters of grief and change. The pastor facilitated a retreat on the topic of reconciliation with his newly formed team, followed by seminars on the universality of the Church as one Body of Christ, which was offered to members of both parishes. These two shared experiences on reconciliation and the mission of the Church prepared the ground for a meeting with members of both parishes to express their concerns and aspirations and discern the way forward. The process was brought to a close with the celebration of the Sacrament of Reconciliation. The reconciliation process facilitated by the pastor allowed members of both parishes to listen to one another and share stories, perspectives, and concerns about the new pastoral situation. The process brought the two parishes closer together and put them on the same page regarding their future under the one pastor. The parishes now share religious education programs, teachers, and a common pastoral team that assists the pastor in developing pastoral plans and programs for both parishes.

Identification of Roles

The bishop made the difficult decision to have one pastor assume responsibility for two different parishes due to a priest shortage situation. Despite geographical proximity to each other, the members of the two parishes in question didn't know one another and had never worked together, thus adding complexity to the situation. The assigned pastor provided timely leadership by listening to concerns from parishioners, appointing a representative team, and setting in motion an effective process of reconciliation. The ten-member reconciliation team worked well with the pastor and with their respective parish communities, thus setting the tone for a prayerful and successful reconciliation process. Learning more about Catholic identity and the mission of the Church gave them a renewed sense of unity in Christ. The leadership from both parishes is willing and ready to share a religious education program and collaborate in other pastoral activities.

Intercultural Competencies Utilized

Knowledge: The pastor understands very well his role as unifier and is able to help members of both parishes better understand the meaning of Catholic identity and the mission of the Church. The process of reconciliation promoted mutual knowledge and understanding among all involved, thus moving beyond stereotypes and prejudice.

Attitudes: The pastor's sense of openness to engage the leadership of both parishes helps create a space of safety and trust among the ten-member reconciliation team. There is openness to new possibilities, risk taking, and moving beyond comfort zones with patience, perseverance, courage, and humility. Everyone has an opportunity to participate and bring ideas, opinions, recommendations, and solutions together. When everyone is involved, there are more chances of bringing an issue to a positive conclusion.

Skills: The ability to create a well-represented team that will develop a reconciliation process and to facilitate it successfully. Listening with openness to one another and making decisions in the context of prayer. The ability to discuss and dialogue, the power of negotiation, and the ability to compromise and to communicate the issues at play in simple terms make the processes of reconciliation and decision making successful.

Pastoral Planning Insight

Identify issues and form a representative team to work with the pastor from the beginning. Develop a process that guarantees high participation and opportunities for open sharing, analysis of issues, prayer, gaining new knowledge, and setting up an inclusive decision-making process that leads to unity and collaboration.

Pastoral Principle

Moving from "us–them" language to "we" language.

Third Pastoral Situation: "Sharing Resources Belonging to All"

Brief description of the pastoral situation

Under the leadership of the pastor, an urban parish made mostly of Americans and African Americans decided to welcome new Catholic Hispanic immigrants into the parish since they realized they were living within the parish boundaries. Once the Sunday Liturgy in Spanish was established, the number of Hispanics attending that Mass grew quite fast and demands for other pastoral services began to emerge, ranging from religious education and prayer groups to social services, among others. The attitude of welcome toward the new community came to a crisis point when complaints from longstanding parishioners about the care of the facilities began to reach the pastor on a consistent basis. The perception that Hispanics were not taking good care of the facilities led some parishioners to suggest that the new hall should not be made available to the Hispanic community and that some kind of signed agreement should be made to make sure that Hispanics knew how to take care of the facilities they were already using. Resentment was growing on both sides as Hispanics began feeling unwelcome and treated unfairly.

Since the parish council had no Hispanic members at the time, the pastor decided to form a well-selected small group of parishioners, representative of the European American, African American, and Hispanic communities, with the sole purpose of assessing the parish facilities and developing criteria for their use and care. The small group began its work by assessing the facilities and developing recommendations for repair and improvements. As a second step, the group identified a number of steps to take good and consistent care of all the facilities, including the new hall, and developed a calendar that was clear and accessible to all parishioners. Once the group finished its work, it made a formal recommendation to the pastor for his review and approval. All parishioners were informed about the commitment of all to the good stewardship of the parish facilities, and signs were made in English and Spanish to remind users of the steps needed in order to *leave the place better than they found it / dejar el lugar mejor de lo que estaba*. The thoughtful sharing of the facilities and the good care for them by all improved significantly as a result of this process.

Identification of Roles

The pastor listened to the legitimate complaints about the importance of taking good care of the parish facilities. He was also keenly aware of the potential unwelcoming attitudes and conflict that could take hold of communities and individuals, particularly around the new hall becoming a symbol of division between the ones who are "in" and the ones who are "out." The representatives from the three communities—African Americans, European Americans, and Hispanics—were well selected by the pastor, and they understood quite well that the mission of the group was not to have one community telling the other what to do or how to do it. Rather, it was to promote a common sense of ownership of the facilities and, therefore, the good care of them. This helped achieve a renewed sense of unity so that the three distinct communities in the parish had access to the decision-making process. All parishioners felt good about taking care of their new hall because it belonged to all of them.

Intercultural Competencies Utilized

Knowledge: The pastor shows a solid understanding of stewardship and the importance of all parishioners having a sense of ownership regarding the facilities of the parish. Knowledge of how different cultures deal with conflict and make decisions was also helpful in putting together the group that assessed the conditions of the facilities and made recommendations to care for them well.

Attitudes: There was openness on the part of the pastor to hear peoples' complaints and to trust that a win-win situation could come out of the impending crisis. Leaders in the appointed group and staff were also open and willing to engage one another without falling into a blame game or into a power struggle.

Skills: Good listening and good intercultural communication among the three different communities; effective use of conflict resolution skills, group dynamics, and the decision-making processes.

Pastoral Planning Insight

Development of a task group with a specific objective, appointed by the pastor, and given authority to make recommendations. The decision-making process was transparent, and each community felt well represented. Thus, everyone embraced the guidelines for good care of facilities.

Pastoral Principle

An inclusive decision-making process leads to a common sense of ownership.

Fourth Pastoral Situation: "Spiritual and Leadership Development"

Brief Description of the Pastoral Situation

The parish was very multicultural and there was a considerable amount of spiritual formation happening within the different language groups. However, there was no cross-cultural program where people could develop both spiritually and as leaders. The parish was offered an opportunity to participate in a 14-week program called *Servant Leadership*. Meeting weekly, the group explored such areas as self-awareness, empowerment, transparency, and community building as they developed a creative and respect-filled style of *servant leadership*. The program created space for people of many different cultures to share what each topic meant to them from the point of view of their culture and history and to have their perspective broadened by the sharing of others and by reading the written thoughts of respected authorities in the area of spirituality and leadership. Over the course of those three months, relationships and a sense of community formed. Most of the participants would go on to serve in leadership positions in the parish, bringing with them their broadened perspective, which would be important especially for those who would eventually go on to serve on the multicultural parish council.

For some, the experience was so powerful that they wanted to share it with others. They were prepared as facilitators and for the next few years shepherded others through the same process that had been so life-giving for them.

Seeing the fruits of this program, two years later, the pastor decided that it would benefit his multicultural staff, so for a year the priests and lay staff participated in the program to deepen their understanding of one another and what it means to be a servant leader.

Identification of Roles

The pastor sees the need to provide spiritual growth and leadership development opportunities for parish leaders from the culturally diverse communities in his parish. He proceeds to identify *Servant Leadership* as a program that covers both areas well and decides to make the investment to bring the program to the parish. Leaders from the various cultural communities respond well to the pastor's invitation to participate in the program and have a very good experience in it. The pastor decides to provide the same opportunity for the priests and lay staff in the parish.

Intercultural Competencies Utilized

Knowledge: The pastor knows that parish leaders are ready to grow spiritually and to develop more leadership skills. He identifies a good resource to provide the formation needed. The pastor also knows how to successfully invite and secure participation of leaders from the various cultural communities in the parish.

Attitudes: Openness to grow spiritually and to develop new skills on the part of the pastor, parish leaders, and staff; openness to share cultural perspectives on the program's content; and openness to develop a sense of community among culturally diverse members. Generous investment of time, talent, and treasure in formation.

Skills: Consultation and research to identify the most suitable program were in place. Organizational skills to set up the training program in terms of space, times, hospitality, and related resources. The program itself improved the skills of participants in terms of self-awareness, empowerment, transparency, and community building as they developed a creative and respect-filled style of servant leadership.

Pastoral Planning Insight

A skilled leadership force is one of the best assets for the development and implementation of pastoral strategies and initiatives. It also builds community and a sense of belonging.

Pastoral Principle

Champion formation and leadership development within each cultural/ethnic community through common experiences.

Fifth Pastoral Situation: "Parish Strategic Planning"

Brief Description of the Pastoral Situation

In 2003–2004 there was a strategic planning process conducted in the parish to develop a pastoral plan for the following three years. Led by an outside facilitator from the diocese, about forty people who were already involved in ministry were gathered. Although the parish was 75 percent immigrant, participation was heavily European American. The people were invited to dream and asked, "What is it we want to see have happened in the parish, in three years?" The large group identified a number of areas, and then people were invited to go to their area of interest and develop an action plan. Some very good things came out of the process, like a multicultural young adult ministry, a revived youth ministry, a new ministry to focus on justice and peace issues, and some renovation in the church building.

In 2008, in a desire to have the process be more collaborative and consultative, a different model was used called Best Practices for Parishes, a program that allows a parish to perform a self-study to "measure" itself against the one hundred most vibrant parishes in the seven key areas of parish life, such as prayer and worship, family and pastoral life, evangelization, and stewardship. Each area had a detailed set of questions in which participants were asked to rate how well their parish performed in a particular area: "Did they do something well, somewhat, rarely, or not at all?"

A consultant was brought in to assist in the process, and a core group was pulled from the parish council to manage the process. Facilitators were trained in the three major languages to conduct these separate self-study listening sessions. People were invited to participate who were currently involved in the ministry and who were not. When the results were compiled, it was discovered that in many areas the rating on a particular question depended on which language group was answering the question. For example, when asked to rate the quality of hospitality at Mass, the French-speaking

Africans with a highly developed hospitality ministry rated it as high, the Latinos who were in the process of forming a ministry rated it somewhere in the middle, and those attending English-speaking Masses rated it as low. On the other hand, in the justice and peace category, the European Americans rated parish efforts "high," the French-speaking "somewhat," and Spanish "rarely." In many other questions, the answer depended on which language group was responding.

The findings of what was done well or not so well was published on the website and then brought to seven open town hall meetings held over the period of six weeks. Each meeting focused on one of the seven areas. Every member of the parish was invited to participate in as many meetings as they liked. The group gathered for prayer and then split into three language groups to recommend, given the findings, what the goals should be in that particular area for the next three years. These recommendations were brought back and shared with the larger group, so that the rationale of each group could be understood. Then the large group made their recommendations. Hundreds of people participated in this stage of the process, and all grew in understanding of the other language communities and their gifts and challenges.

When the seven meetings were over, the recommendations went to the multicultural parish council, and they prioritized, chose the goals, and developed an action plan with timelines and responsibilities. Summaries were published in the bulletin and the complete 74-page plan was placed permanently on the parish website.

Because the process was consultative at each level there was more understanding of what the parish was trying to achieve, more of a sense of mission in the parish, a greater understanding of its diversity and complexity, and ultimately more of a sense of ownership of the plan.

Pastoral Principle

Plan with people, not for people.

Exercise: Identify Your Own Best Practice

Following the outline used in the five pastoral situations, which showed particular best practices, identify a pastoral situation in your parish that was addressed in such a way that the response can be considered a best practice.

- **a)** Brief description of the pastoral situation
- **b)** Identification of roles
- **c)** Intercultural competencies utilized: knowledge, attitudes, and skills
- **d)** Insight for pastoral planning
- **e)** Pastoral principle

Conclusion

Parish life is the privileged context in which Catholics experience a personal and a communal encounter with Christ. It is also the spiritual home where the faithful develop a sense of belonging in the Church and where they engage in ministries of service to one another and to the broader community. The emergence of thousands of *shared parishes* over the past few decades is a pastoral response to a major population shift taking place in dioceses across the country. Shared parishes are also a *sign of the times,* calling Catholics from different races, cultures, and ethnicities to experience anew the spirit of Pentecost, so we can hear and understand one another, moved by the same spirit of love and nurtured at the one Eucharistic Table of the Lord.

However, building unity in diversity requires particular attitudes, knowledge, and skills. It also requires having a clear and profoundly ecclesial understanding of what we want to achieve in our shared parishes and how we actually want to do it. We are grateful that the spirit of unity and pastoral love has inspired many pastors and their teams to achieve high levels of ecclesial integration/inclusion among the culturally diverse members in their shared parishes.

The stories, pastoral principles, and practical recommendations included in this guide are a great resource for thousands of pastors entrusted with the pastoral care of shared parishes and for others who may find themselves ministering in a shared parish in the future. The guide is also helpful for staff and parish leaders collaborating with the pastor in the wonderful and yet difficult task of building unity in diversity. Along with the practical examples and insights, the guide provides a methodology for understanding the process of intercultural sensitivity and healthy integration. This methodology is interpreted through a spirituality of ministry and a sense of Catholic identity based in Scripture that has inspired and guided the work of many pastors of shared parishes and their teams.

We are keenly aware that the work for the New Evangelization is being carried out in shared parishes in a unique way as we become missionaries to one another and honor the presence of Christ in our diverse cultures. May we become ever more united at the Eucharistic Table of the Lord in our parishes and other Catholic institutions, and may we echo in our lives the prayer of Christ for us all, **"SO THAT THEY MAY ALL BE ONE."**

Mejores prácticas en parroquias compartidas

Para que todos sean uno

Comité de Diversidad Cultural en la Iglesia
CONFERENCIA DE OBISPOS CATÓLICOS DE LOS ESTADOS UNIDOS
WASHINGTON, DC

El documento *Para que todos sean uno: Guía práctica para párrocos y equipos de parroquias compartidas* fue elaborado como un recurso por el Comité de Diversidad Cultural en la Iglesia de la Conferencia de Obispos Católicos de los Estados Unidos (USCCB). Éste fue revisado por el obispo Daniel Flores, presidente del comité, y ha sido autorizado para su publicación por el suscrito.

Monseñor Ronny Jenkins
Secretario General, USCCB

Las ilustraciones en las páginas 66, 69 y 74 por Carmen Fernández.

Imagen de la portada, "Jesus the Word," copyright © 2014 Michele Hehenberger, cortesía de Das Grup, Inc. Utilizado con permiso. Todos los derechos reservados.

La cita del papa Juan Pablo II, *Ecclesia in America*, copyright © 1999, Libreria Editrice Vaticana (LEV), Cuidad del Vaticano; La cita del papa Francis, Homilía, 14 de marzo de 2013, copyright © 2013, LEV. Todos los derechos reservados.

Citas del *Código de Derecho Canónico: Edición Latín-Español*, Vaticano, han sido impresas con permiso. Todos los derechos reservados.

Los textos de la Sagrada Escritura utilizados en esta obra han sido tomados de los *Leccionarios I, II y III*, propiedad de la Comisión Episcopal de Pastoral Litúrgica de la Conferencia Episcopal Mexicana, copyright © 1987, quinta edición de septiembre de 2011. Utilizados con permiso. Todos los derechos reservados.

Los textos de *Biblia de América*, 6ª edición, copyright © 1994, La Casa de la Biblia, Madrid.

Copyright © 2013, United States Conference of Catholic Bishops, Washington, DC. Todos los derechos reservados. Esta obra no se puede reproducir, en su totalidad o en cualquier parte por ningún medio, electrónico o mecánico, lo cual incluye fotocopias, grabaciones, o cualquier método de almacenamiento, sin permiso escrito del propietario de los derechos.

Mejores prácticas en parroquias compartidas: Para que todos sean uno

Reconocimientos: Agradecemos a los veinte párrocos que aportaron su tiempo, conocimiento y experiencia a la elaboración de este recurso para el ministerio parroquial. Su sensibilidad pastoral y recomendaciones prácticas constituyen el fundamento de esta guía. Es más, su celo apostólico y su capacidad de reunir a personas de distintas culturas y etnias como una única comunidad parroquial de fe son una auténtica inspiración para párrocos y líderes pastorales de todo Estados Unidos. Agradecemos también a Carmen Aguinaco por reunir las experiencias y contribuciones de los párrocos y a Brett Hoover, PhD, por desarrollar el documento que sirvió como fundamento para esta guía. De modo especial, agradecemos al Rev. Stephen Dudek, al Rev. Michael Johnson, OFM, y al Rev. Héctor Madrigal por acompañar el desarrollo de la guía desde sus estados iniciales hasta la articulación final.

Origen: En 2007, los obispos católicos de Estados Unidos seleccionaron la diversidad cultural en la Iglesia en una de las cinco prioridades principales de su plan estratégico, para responder mejor a la creciente realidad de las parroquias y diócesis de Estados Unidos de América. El grupo timón de USCCB que trabajaba en esta prioridad recomendó el desarrollo de una guía práctica para ayudar a los párrocos de parroquias culturalmente diversas en la desafiante tarea de construir unidad en la diversidad. Tal guía se consideraba urgente e importante ya que el número de parroquias compartidas por comunidades diversas había crecido dramáticamente en la década precedente, de un 22 por ciento en 2000 al 33 por ciento en 2010.

Se pidió al Comité de Diversidad Cultural en la Iglesia que jugara un papel esencial en el desarrollo de la guía, a través de una consulta con párrocos que han logrado con éxito un alto nivel de integración/inclusión eclesial entre sus feligreses de diversas procedencias culturales. Veinte párrocos de distintos orígenes étnicos y regiones del país fueron consultados en un período de diez y ocho meses. Las recomendaciones finales para la guía se hicieron en diciembre de 2012, incluido el título: *Mejores prácticas en parroquias compartidas: Para que todos sean uno.*

El término "parroquias compartidas" designa comunidades parroquiales en las que están presentes dos o más idiomas o contextos culturales en la vida ministerial de una parroquia. El término fue acuñado por Brett Hoover y ha sido adoptado para su uso en esta guía.

Finalidad: La finalidad de la guía es asistir a los párrocos de parroquias compartidas y a sus equipos para lograr un alto nivel de integración eclesial entre feligreses pertenecientes a diversas culturas. Está diseñada como instrumento práctico para (a) evaluar situaciones pastorales desafiantes a la luz de los principios y valores pastorales católicos; (b) identificar respuestas pastorales para manejar situaciones pastorales basándose en prácticas óptimas comprobadas; (c) aplicar capacidades interculturales internamente en forma de actitudes, conocimiento y destrezas; y (d) discernir estrategias de planificación pastoral basadas en un proceso de desarrollo de integración/inclusión eclesial y sensibilidad intercultural, que puedan llevar a un más alto nivel de sentido de corresponsabilidad.

Metodología: La guía tiene tres partes. La primera parte describe los seis pasos de sensibilidad intercultural desarrollados por Milton Bennett y cómo estos se aplican a una parroquia enfrentada al desafío de responder a cambios demográficos dentro de sus confines. La Parte I ilustra cómo un párroco y su personal podrían pasar por distintas fases de comprensión de su misión, en su intento por responder a una nueva realidad. Los pasos de sensibilidad intercultural de Bennett describen cómo enfrentarse a cambios demográficos podría incluir pasar por un proceso de negación, ponerse a la defensiva y minimizar la diversidad cultural emergente en medio de nosotros, antes de pasar a un proceso de aceptar, adaptar e integrar esa nueva realidad. La Parte I también incluye experiencias pastorales que ilustran las mejores prácticas de algunas de las parroquias compartidas que participaron en la consulta.

La Parte II articula el concepto católico de parroquia y los principios y valores pastorales que orientan la vida y misión de las parroquias católicas. Tal comprensión hace volverse nuestra reflexión desde las implicaciones sociológicas de la diversidad cultural a la misión de la Iglesia Católica según la expresa el derecho canónico y recibe luz de la identidad más profunda de la Iglesia, es decir, de su misión evangelizadora. También refleja la espiritualidad ministerial del párroco y su equipo al responder a los desafíos de una creciente diversidad cultural en el espíritu de la Nueva Evangelización. La metodología cristiana de encuentro con el Jesucristo vivo como camino de conversión, comunión y solidaridad, según se expresa en la Exhortación Apostólica *Ecclesia in America*, proporciona el marco de referencia para la Parte II.

La Parte III ofrece un mapa de ruta de tres encrucijadas que ilustra cómo las parroquias han logrado construir la unidad en la diversidad entre los feligreses pertenecientes a diversos grupos culturales. Estas tres encrucijadas son *bienvenida, pertenencia* y *posesión*. Describen el proceso de desarrollo para la integración/inclusión eclesial que quisiéramos lograr en el creciente número de parroquias compartidas, "para que todos sean uno" (Jn 17:21). Las tres encrucijadas de integración/inclusión se describen a través de nueve movimientos o indicadores. Más tarde, los movimientos son ilustrados por situaciones reales de ministerio que los párrocos y sus equipos han manejado con éxito. Los párrocos que participaron en la consulta estaban de acuerdo en que un mayor nivel de integración/inclusión eclesial entre los feligreses tiene como resultado un nivel más alto de corresponsabilidad y misión.

Movimientos o indicadores de desarrollo: La guía ofrece nueve indicadores de desarrollo o movimientos como claves para medir el nivel de integración/inclusión eclesial en una parroquia compartida concreta y que sirven para discernir los pasos sucesivos. Incluyen principios pastorales y capacidades interculturales relevantes para el nivel de integración/inclusión eclesial necesario en cada uno de los movimientos. Los primeros tres movimientos son esenciales para la encrucijada del sentido de *bienvenida*. Los movimientos 4, 5 y 6 son el fruto del sentido de *pertenencia*. Los movimientos 7, 8 y 9 son una expresión del sentido de *corresponsabilidad*:

Bienvenida

- Misión
- Regreso al hogar
- Crecimiento ministerial

Pertenencia

- Construir relaciones a través de las culturas
- Desarrollo y formación del liderazgo intercultural
- Proceso de toma de decisiones

Corresponsabilidad

- Compartir recursos
- Lograr corresponsabilidad
- Comunión en misión

Cómo usar esta guía: Esta guía se puede utilizar como instrumento para entrenar al personal parroquial y a líderes en el proceso de integración/inclusión eclesial.

La Parte I se centra en las fases de sensibilidad intercultural. Está dirigida a ayudar al personal parroquial y a los líderes a evaluar su propio nivel de sensibilidad intercultural y a discernir cómo pueden avanzar en tal proceso. Podría ser útil proporcionar datos sobre la demografía de la parroquia como un buen punto de arranque para la sesión. La Parte II se puede llevar a cabo en modo de retiro para maximizar los beneficios de un contenido espiritual tan rico. Una espiritualidad de hospitalidad y reconciliación son el núcleo de la Parte II, ya que trata de temas de encuentro personal, conversión, comunión y solidaridad en Cristo.

La Parte III se puede presentar como proceso de desarrollo que evalúe dos realidades diferentes. Una de ellas es el nivel de integración/inclusión eclesial logrado en la parroquia hasta el momento. La otra es el nivel de capacidad intercultural que ha conseguido cada miembro del personal y cada líder parroquial en términos de actitudes, conocimiento y destrezas.

El entrenamiento se puede realizar de distintas maneras. Se puede hacer, por ejemplo, como un día de formación, o como una serie de tres tardes, dedicando una tarde a cada parte de la guía.

La guía se puede usar también como instrumento de planificación pastoral para ayudar a discernir los siguientes pasos a dar en una parroquia concreta para que pueda llegar a ser más competente interculturalmente y a estar mejor integrada en el sentido católico de la palabra.

PARTE I

Parroquias compartidas y sensibilidad intercultural

¿Qué son las parroquias compartidas y cómo llegan a serlo? El término "parroquias compartidas" describe las comunidades parroquiales en las que dos o más idiomas o contextos culturales son parte integral de la vida y misión de una parroquia concreta. Un ejemplo de parroquia compartida es San Camilo, en Silver Spring, Maryland, donde la liturgia dominical se celebra en inglés, francés y español, así como en el contexto espiritual y cultural de la comunidad afroamericana. Estas cuatro comunidades étnicas y culturales comparten la vida y la misión de una sola comunidad parroquial. La educación religiosa, pastoral juvenil y otros ministerios también se ofrecen en distintos idiomas, pero están organizados y coordinados bajo una única visión para la educación religiosa, pastoral juvenil, etc. La parroquia San Camilo ha sido parroquia compartida durante varios años y ha logrado un alto nivel de integración eclesial a través de una identidad católica comúnmente compartida. Pero eso no fue siempre así. Durante muchos años, San Camilo fue una comunidad homogénea de una mayoría de católicos acomodados de origen europeo. Fue un cambio demográfico lo que desafió al párroco de San Camilo y a su equipo a responder a los grupos culturalmente diversos, cada vez más grandes, que vivían dentro de los límites parroquiales.

Hoy día, un 33 por ciento de las parroquias de Estados Unidos son parroquias compartidas, comparado con el 22 por ciento del año 2000. Se espera que el número de parroquias compartidas crezca significativamente en un futuro inmediato, a medida que siguen dándose cambios demográficos, la mayoría debidos al influjo de los nuevos inmigrantes católicos del hemisferio sur. La consolidación de las parroquias es otro factor en el número creciente de parroquias compartidas.

La transición de una parroquia culturalmente homogénea a una parroquia compartida no es una tarea fácil. Algunos de los factores que frenan a los feligreses en su acogida a sus hermanos católicos de distintas culturas y etnias pueden ser un sentido de incertidumbre, el temor a lo desconocido, la sensación de escasez, la capacidad intercultural limitada y una cierta tendencia a querer asimilar a la gente para que sean "como nosotros". La tendencia a considerar a la parroquia como congregación, en lugar de como territorio, según lo define el derecho canónico, también es un impedimento.

Seis fases de sensibilidad intercultural

Varios de los párrocos que participaron en la consulta para desarrollar esta guía se refirieron al modelo de Milton Bennett, *six stages of intercultural sensitivity* como un instrumento útil para comprender por lo que pasan los párrocos y sus equipos en su esfuerzo por responder a los cambios demográficos. Las seis fases son: negación, defensa, minimización, adaptación e integración, y describen el modo en que una persona o una organización pasan de resistirse a la relación con personas de una cultura distinta a estar abiertos y ser capaces de trabajar, relacionarse y colaborar con poblaciones culturalmente diversas. Las fases son también útiles para los párrocos y el personal que ya están sirviendo en parroquias compartidas y que en ocasiones se pueden encontrar a sí mismos como atascados en el proceso de desarrollo de la integración/inclusión.

Lo siguiente es un ejemplo de una parroquia que ha sido culturalmente homogénea y que pasa por los procesos de sensibilidad intercultural mencionados. El ejemplo muestra un barrio en el que el número de nuevos inmigrantes haitianos dentro de los límites geográficos de la parroquia ha crecido significativamente. El párroco/administrador y el personal no son conscientes de esta presencia creciente y no tienen experiencia en trabajar con inmigrantes haitianos.

Fase 1. Negativa

Se le pregunta al párroco sobre la presencia de nuevos inmigrantes haitianos en su parroquia. El párroco responde: *No tenemos haitianos en la parroquia.* Añade que hay unas cuantas familias haitianas pero, *son como todos y han sido feligreses por mucho tiempo*. El párroco y su personal se sienten muy sorprendidos cuando escuchan los datos del Censo de 2010 que muestran que hay más de trescientas familias haitianas que viven en los límites de la parroquia. El párroco y el personal podrían mantenerse en esta negación, aduciendo que esas personas están simplemente de paso, que no son necesariamente católicas, o que podrían ser "ilegales". En esta fase de negativa, la gente tiende a no ver al "otro" o a considerar al "otro" como la responsabilidad de otras personas.

Fase 2. Defensa

Una vez que el párroco y su personal se han hecho conscientes de la presencia de una comunidad de católicos a los que no se está llegando o incluyendo, existe una tendencia a racionalizar las razones por las que "esa gente" no está siendo incluida. Las razones que se dan pueden incluir algunos de los siguientes argumentos: *Ya no hay sitio en esta parroquia. ¿Son de fiar? ¡Van a invadir! No son como nosotros; mis abuelos construyeron esta parroquia. Se deberían ir a la parroquia de al lado*. Estas razones están motivadas por el temor a lo desconocido. No tienen intención necesariamente de ser hirientes o racistas, pero a menudo se originan en estereotipos que pueden resultar discriminatorios.

Fase 3. Minimización

El párroco y su equipo son conscientes del creciente número de familias haitianas que viven dentro de los límites de la parroquia y reconocen que la responsabilidad de la parroquia es responder. Sin embargo, hay un impulso de minimizar las diferencias para no tener que cambiar el modo en que se hacen las cosas en la parroquia. Por ejemplo, los argumentos en esta fase podrían ser algo como: *Pueden participar si así lo desean, la puerta está abierta de par en par;* o *Ahora viven en Estados Unidos y deberían aprender inglés y asimilarse como todo el mundo*. Esta respuesta comienza a mostrar un cierto grado de apertura a dar la bienvenida a las personas, pero solo hasta el punto en que las cosas no cambien en "nuestra parroquia" y ellos dejen atrás su lengua, cultura, tradiciones y expectativas. La expresión "daltónico" encaja aquí en sentido literal, ya que la gente opta por no ver las diferencias con los demás. Sin embargo, la intención es justificar el no tener que hacer nada distinto, sino esperar a que el otro encaje en "nuestro" modo de pensar y "nuestro" modo de hacer las cosas. Establecer una liturgia dominical en creole se considera innecesario, e incluso se podría percibir como divisorio. Esta fase es especialmente difícil de superar cuando se refiere a la formación en la fe de los niños y jóvenes de poblaciones inmigrantes nuevas. El hecho de que los hijos de los inmigrantes sepan inglés, o estén en proceso de aprenderlo, deja fuera de la ecuación diferencias significativas como cultura, raza, logros educativos, estatus social y económico y estatus migratorio, entre otras cosas.

Fase 4. Aceptación

En esta fase el párroco y el personal reconocen las diferencias como bastante reales y saben que la misma conducta podría significar distintas cosas para personas de culturas diferentes. Existe la voluntad de cambiar la perspectiva mientras que se mantiene el compromiso con "nuestros propios valores". Establecer una liturgia dominical en creole puede estar bien mientras no moleste a otros y ellos cuiden bien de "nuestras cosas". En esta fase, la comunidad establecida y la nueva comunidad haitiana podrían compartir edificios, estacionamiento y templo, pero a distintas horas y evitando encontrarse unos con otros. Un ministro sacramental de otra parroquia podría presidir la liturgia dominical en creole con un contacto mínimo con el párroco y su personal. Hay un sentido de tratar al otro con educación, pero persiste el lenguaje de "nosotros/ellos".

Fase 5. Adaptación

En la fase de adaptación, el párroco y su personal son capaces de entender y simpatizar con distintas perspectivas y de adaptar su conducta de acuerdo con esta nueva comprensión. El párroco, su personal y el liderazgo de la comunidad inmigrante han desarrollado capacidades interculturales significativas, tales como la habilidad de comunicarse en dos idiomas, establecer relaciones interpersonales a través de las culturas, y una apertura a nuevas ideas y proyectos que se originan en una comunidad concreta. Hay un sentido de que ambas comunidades pertenecen a la parroquia y que la gente está más dispuesta a relacionarse, trabajar y colaborar unos con otros. Se utiliza el lenguaje de "nosotros" entre el liderazgo de ambas comunidades. Hay una variedad de programas y proyectos disponibles en ambos idiomas y se han hecho cambios para incluir las necesidades de la comunidad haitiana, dentro de ciertos límites. Trasladar la liturgia dominical en creole a una hora mejor, o permitir actividades de recaudación de fondos para actividades y programas específicos haitianos son cambios significativos en la vida de la parroquia. Sin embargo, en esta fase aún no hay un alto grado de participación por parte de la comunidad inmigrante en los centros de toma de decisiones de la parroquia, como puede ser el consejo parroquial, el consejo financiero o el personal.

Fase 6. Integración

En esta fase el párroco, su equipo y el liderazgo de la comunidad haitiana pasan con naturalidad de un marco de referencia cultural a otro, adaptándose a distintas situaciones con facilidad y acierto cultural. El liderazgo de ambas comunidades culturales tiene un sentido de posesión de la parroquia. Hay una buena representación de ambas culturas en todos los centros de decisión y el personal parroquial, y los recursos se generan y comparten según las necesidades y aspiraciones de ambas comunidades en la parroquia.

Las tres áreas de capacidad cultural

El desarrollo de una sensibilidad intercultural requiere la adquisición de capacidad intercultural para el ministerio. La capacidad intercultural es la capacidad de comunicarse, relacionarse y trabajar cruzando fronteras culturales. Implica desarrollar capacidad en tres áreas: *conocimiento, destrezas* y *actitudes.*

El conocimiento implica la capacidad de entender más de una sola perspectiva sobre cómo se hacen las cosas. Entender cómo toman decisiones las distintas comunidades culturales, cómo utilizan el tiempo durante sus reuniones, con cuánta anticipación planifican, cómo recaudan fondos para la parroquia, cómo preparan y celebran la liturgia, etc., permite al ministro intercultural facilitar la comunicación, organización y puesta en marcha de actividades parroquiales comunes. El *conocimiento* favorece el enfoque de "ambos-y" sobre el de "un tamaño para todos".

Las destrezas incluyen la habilidad de comunicarse en más de una lengua, de simpatizar con feligreses de distintas culturas y experiencias, escuchar bien y motivar a la gente para que participe activamente en los diversos ministerios de la parroquia. También incluye la capacidad de facilitar reuniones, dirigir entrenamientos, coordinar voluntarios, manejar conflictos y proporcionar apoyo a líderes de distintas culturas. *Las destrezas* convierten al ministro en "mentor intercultural", que sabe cómo "planificar con la gente y no para la gente".

Las actitudes incluyen la apertura para inspirar en los feligreses de distintas culturas

CAPICIDADES INTERCULTURALES

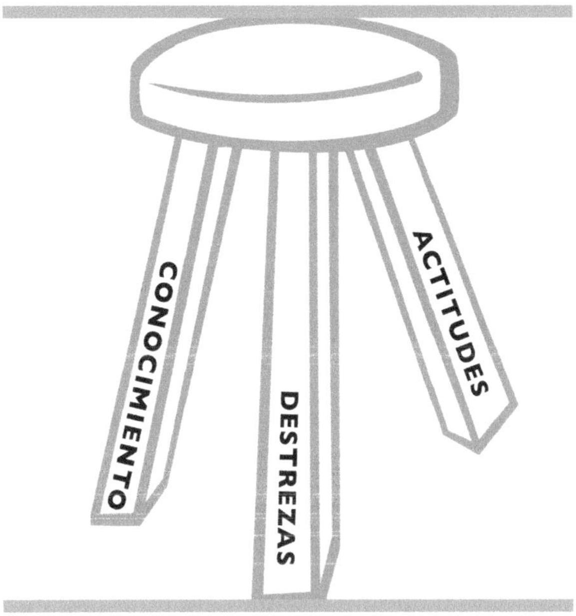

un sentido de gratitud y curiosidad. Hace que la gente se sienta en casa y es eficaz en construir relaciones entre las culturas que conducen a la aceptación mutua, la valoración y la colaboración. Las *actitudes* describen al ministro como "constructor de puentes" capaz de reunir a la gente y motivarla a contribuir sus talentos especiales para el bien de todos y de la misión común de la parroquia.

Considere las siguientes preguntas para ver dónde se encuentran usted y el liderazgo de su parroquia en la línea de la sensibilidad intercultural y en el área de capacidad intercultural:

a) ¿Ha experimentado su parroquia un cambio demográfico significativo en los últimos años?
b) ¿Cómo ha respondido su parroquia a este cambio de población?
c) ¿Qué fase de sensibilidad intercultural describe mejor dónde se sitúan usted y su personal en esta línea?
d) ¿Qué capacidades interculturales —conocimiento, actitudes y destrezas— practican el párroco, el personal y los líderes parroquiales?
e) ¿Qué aspectos impiden al liderazgo de la parroquia lograr la siguiente fase de sensibilidad intercultural o de capacidad intercultural?

Historias desde la trinchera

Las seis fases de sensibilidad intercultural y las tres áreas de capacidad intercultural son muy útiles para entender el proceso para alcanzar la unidad en la diversidad. Las fases también son útiles para identificar los objetivos claves y capacidades a medida que pasamos por el proceso. Sin embargo, cuando hablamos sobre ministerio, tanto la espiritualidad como el compromiso con el bien de la persona humana reclaman una dimensión añadida de responsabilidad mutua. Tal dimensión viene del hecho de que la misión de la Iglesia es precisamente llevar la Buena Noticia de Jesucristo a toda situación humana. También nos llama a acogernos unos a otros y a ser los guardianes de la dignidad de toda persona humana, y especialmente de los más vulnerables de entre nosotros.

A continuación se presentan historias de parroquias compartidas que han acogido la llamada a salir al encuentro de las poblaciones étnica y culturalmente diversas que viven dentro de sus límites. En algunos casos, los párrocos y sus equipos eran conscientes de las fases de sensibilidad cultural y capacidad intercultural y las usaron para navegar las aguas ambiguas de las relaciones interculturales. En algunos casos, simplemente siguieron su intuición pastoral y un buen grado de sentido común y solidaridad. Sin embargo, el ingrediente muy presente en todos los casos fue el celo apostólico por parte del párroco y su equipo de cumplir el mandato eclesial de llevar la Buena Noticia de Jesucristo a todas las comunidades étnicas y culturales bajo su cuidado pastoral. Después de una consulta con los párrocos de veinte parroquias compartidas, ofrecemos las siguientes viñetas de algunas de las parroquias compartidas que funcionan bien en el país.

La parroquia de San Francisco de Sales está ubicada en una comunidad suburbana al Oeste de Grand Rapids, Michigan, en una ciudad llamada Holland. Allí, feligreses hispanos, vietnamitas y estadounidenses de ascendencia europea comparten San Francisco como hogar espiritual. En 1995, se produjo un incendio en la parroquia en el día de la Fiesta de Nuestra Señora de Guadalupe. El área de culto quedó prácticamente destruida. Antes de la demolición, la parroquia entró en un período de luto comunitario. "Velaron" a la iglesia, como dijo el que era entonces párroco, el P. Stephen Dudek. Recuerda Dudek: "La gente llegaba al espacio quemado para presentar flores, encender velas y compartir recuerdos". Después, la gente de las tres comunidades trabajó junta, codo a codo con martillos y cinceles para salvar unos 10,000 ladrillos de la ruina. Esos ladrillos serían más tarde incorporados a la iglesia reconstruida. Se formaron "grupos reactores" de las tres comunidades y todos contribuyeron sus ideas al nuevo diseño. La iglesia reconstruida contenía arte sacro de las tres tradiciones culturales y fue construida en redondo para enfatizar la igualdad entre ellas.

La parroquia de San José en Amarillo, Texas, combina una comunidad de más edad, de clase media, méxicoamericana y euroamericana, con inmigrantes hispanos más jóvenes y refugiados de Sudán y Bosnia. Cuando un nuevo párroco, el P. Héctor Madrigal, llegó en 2007, llevó a cabo sesiones de escucha y aprendió directamente sobre muchas de las divisiones dentro de la parroquia, la mayoría de ellas enfocadas en la competición entre distintas escuelas locales, católicas y públicas. Las sesiones de escucha llevaron a una *alianza* o pacto en el que todos los grupos comunitarios hicieron un compromiso de trabajar por la unidad en Cristo. Celebraron esta alianza con un servicio de sanación y luego con la primera Misa de la unidad de la parroquia, celebrada bajo una carpa fuera del templo. Todos los distintos grupos de la parroquia entraron en la tienda en procesión y firmaron la alianza en presencia del obispo de la diócesis. Todos los años la parroquia lleva a cabo una ceremonia de renovación con otra Misa multilingüe en el exterior de la iglesia. También honran una piedra de "unidad en Cristo" colocada cerca de la entrada del templo para recordar a todos de su compromiso mutuo en presencia de Dios.

San Camilo, en Silver Spring, Maryland, es el tipo de parroquia compartida que hace tambalearse a la imaginación de la mayoría de los católicos. Dirigida por frailes franciscanos, la parroquia está ubicada en los suburbios más cultural y socioeconómicamente diversos del área metropolitana de Washington, D.C. Acoge a casi cinco mil personas en Misa cada fin de semana. El grupo más grande de la parroquia es la comunidad centroamericana, la mayoría de El Salvador y Guatemala. Veinticinco por ciento de los feligreses son nuevos inmigrantes anglo o francés parlantes de África, un quinto son estadounidenses de origen europeo; hay también una comunidad afroamericana y una comunidad de personas bengalís (originalmente de Bangladesh). Bajo el liderazgo del P. Michael Johnson, OFM, el personal de la parroquia representa a todos los grupos y la Misa se celebra los domingos en tres idiomas (español, inglés y francés). Hay liturgias trilingües en seis festividades, además de Navidad y durante el Triduo Pascual. Se reza el rosario en cinco idiomas todas las mañanas. Un diversidad de movimientos eclesiales laicos (como el movimiento de renovación carismático y el movimiento de retiros SEARCH) encuentran su hogar en San Camilo. Los feligreses están involucrados (a menudo juntos) en setenta y dos ministerios distintos, incluyendo catequesis, evangelización, ministerios litúrgicos y juveniles, organizaciones de justicia y servicio social, entre otras cosas. Un comité también promueve "Cuidado de la Creación", o preocupaciones ecológicas en la radio en español.

Yuba City es una pequeña ciudad en el Valle de Sacramento, en el norte de California. El valle es rico en agricultura. Ahí está **la parroquia San Isidro**. En San Isidro, como en la mayoría de California, las personas euroamericanas no constituyen la mayoría. La parroquia tiene cuatro misas en inglés y tres en español, pero los que asisten en español son una ligera mayoría. La educación religiosa se imparte en ambos idiomas, utilizando un libro bilingüe bajo la dirección de un director de educación religiosa que es bilingüe. El Fondo de San Francisco de Asís de la parroquia ayuda a personas pobres y sin hogar de cualquier origen. Dos veces al año, más de cien voluntarios de las comunidades hispana, euroamericana y filipina unen fuerzas para celebrar grandes cenas para personas sin hogar de la zona, y tales cenas se convierten en una de las muchas expresiones de unidad en la diversidad, según el P. Francisco Hernández, párroco de la iglesia.

Schaumburg, Illinois, es un suburbio lejano del área de Chicago y es diverso en términos socioeconómicos y culturales. La **Iglesia del Espíritu Santo** acoge a una comunidad multicultural de euroamericanos, hispanos (la mayoría mexicanos) y filipinos, con unos cuantos inmigrantes de otras nacionalidades. El consejo parroquial lleva a cabo reuniones abiertas cinco veces al año para asegurarse de que todos los feligreses tienen voz en los asuntos parroquiales. El párroco, P. William Tkachuk, atribuye el éxito de la parroquia a la "voluntad por parte de los líderes parroquiales de los distintos grupos étnicos de continuar desarrollando y fomentando estructuras y actividades que nutren la visión de la parroquia de un Cuerpo de Cristo con muchos miembros diversos", una visión arraigada en la unidad en la diversidad de la Santísima Trinidad. La parroquia trabaja activamente por los derechos de los inmigrantes. Y sin embargo, el P. Bill admite que algunas personas no aprecian las liturgias bilingües que

PREGUNTAS PARA LA REFLEXIÓN

1) ¿Cuáles son algunos puntos comunes que se encuentran en estas parroquias compartidas?
2) ¿Qué valores evangélicos se ven resaltar?
3) ¿Qué desafíos y oportunidades pueden identificar?
4) ¿De qué modos le inspiran a usted en su ministerio?
5) ¿Qué fase de sensibilidad intercultural piensa que se ha logrado en cada parroquia?

se celebran el Jueves Santo y en otros días de fiesta. Recuerda que un feligrés le dijo un día: "¿Por qué tenemos que tenerlo en dos lenguas? No me gusta". El párroco respondió: "No hay nada malo en que no te guste". Reconoció francamente la dificultad para quienes no son bilingües. "Pero el incluir los idiomas de todos es la exigencia del evangelio", añade. "No estamos intentando ser políticamente correctos, sino vivir el evangelio. No nos tiene que gustar para estar comprometidos a hacerlo".

Por otro lado, los feligreses de **Nuestra Señora de Lourdes** parecen disfrutar sus liturgias bilingües que tienen lugar de vez en cuando. Ubicada en Montclair, en el condado Inland Empire, al este de Los Ángeles, California, la parroquia está dividida en cuartos casi iguales—mexicanos y centroamericanos, suramericanos, euroamericanos, y asiáticos. Un año de educación sobre las celebraciones bilingües ayudaron a formar una mística común, que se resume en la declaración de misión: "Abrazamos la misión de Jesús y buscamos construir el cuerpo de Cristo y traer a todos el mundo, todas las razas y todos los grupos étnicos a la plena unión con Él. Caminamos juntos en fe y nos esforzamos por ser una familia orante y eucarística". El párroco, P. Anthony Dao, dice que el invitar regularmente a las distintas comunidades a servirse unas a otras en diversos acontecimientos ayuda a cimentar las relaciones entre las comunidades culturales. Pero también nota que todos deben tener cuidado de no esperar demasiado inmediatamente.

Finalmente, como indica el P. Stephen Dudek, se dan asuntos de diversidad e inclusión no solamente entre las culturas—latino, vietnamita, sudanés, etc—sino también entre las categorías más amplias y las familias culturales mismas. Utiliza como ejemplo la diversidad de culturas latinas o hispanas presentes en su parroquia actual. En **San José Obrero**, han empezado a celebrar la novena en honor de Nuestra Señora del Rosario—la advocación bajo la que los guatemaltecos honran a María—al mismo tiempo que la novena en honor de Nuestra Señora de Guadalupe. Esto, a su vez, inspiró a la comunidad puertorriqueña a dar nueva vida a su novena a Nuestra

Señora Madre de la Divina Providencia. Así mismo, para la creciente comunidad guatemalteca, se añadió otra novena en enero en honor del *Cristo Negro de Esquipulas*. Para la fiesta de Nuestra Señora de la Caridad del Cobre—la advocación bajo la que los cubanos honran a María—tuvieron una cena cubana después de la Misa y fue la primera vez que los feligreses guatemaltecos habían comido comida cubana. Estos tipos de interacciones con las diversas comunidades son también importantes de recordar.

PARTE II

La comprensión católica de la vida parroquial y la misión

La parroquia católica

Según las contribuciones recibidas de los párrocos implicados en la consulta, un número significativo de personal parroquial y líderes consideran la parroquia más como congregación, esto es, un grupo de católicos inscritos que están implicados en diversos grados en la vida de la parroquia. Tal comprensión de la parroquia a menudo se basa en la experiencia de fieles católicos bien establecidos que se han conocido por mucho tiempo. Este concepto congregacional se parece más a una comunidad de fe protestante americana que centra la vida cristiana en quienes *voluntariamente* se reúnen para el culto. Por contraste, la Iglesia Católica define la parroquia en varios modos distintos que no son mutuamente excluyentes. Por ejemplo, el canon 515 dice: "La parroquia es una determinada comunidad de fieles cristianos constituida de modo estable en la Iglesia particular," y el canon 518 establece que: "como regla general, la parroquia ha de ser territorial, es decir, ha de comprender a todos los fieles cristianos de un territorio determinado". La última definición ve a la parroquia como un territorio con límites geográficos bien marcados.

Según el derecho canónico, el párroco es responsable por el bienestar spiritual de todos los que viven dentro de los límites parroquiales definidos, y no sólo de los que están inscritos. Como tal, el párroco y su equipo están llamados a un ministerio constante de misión que se esfuerza por llevar la Buena Noticia de Jesucristo a toda situación humana presente en la parroquia. El papel evangelizador del párroco está explicitado en el derecho canónico, así como en la naturaleza misionera de la Iglesia. El bienestar espiritual de los fieles es un elemento esencial. La llamada a una Nueva

Evangelización adquiere mucho más sentido cuando pensamos en la parroquia como territorio. El párroco y su equipo pueden generar toda clase de posibilidades y oportunidades, al buscar modos nuevos y creativos de salir al encuentro de todos los católicos bautizados y de otros que viven en los límites parroquiales y no solo de los ya congregados.

Es importante advertir que es muy aceptable que los católicos sean miembros de una parroquia incluso si viven fuera de los límites de esa parroquia concreta. Esta práctica está ampliamente utilizada en Estados Unidos y con resultados pastorales muy buenos. La práctica, sin embargo, no excusa la responsabilidad del párroco y su equipo de responder a las necesidades pastorales y aspiraciones de la gente que vive dentro de los límites de esa parroquia. Hemos de recordar también que algunas parroquias no son territoriales, tales como las afiliadas a colegios y universidades, establecimientos militares y algunas parroquias étnicas.

Las parroquias compartidas presentan desafíos significativos, pero ofrecen mayores oportunidades de involucrarse en profundas conversaciones sobre la vida y la fe: de dar culto y orar juntos, de aprender unos de otros, de apoyarnos unos a otros, de perdonarse mutuamente y reconciliarse, de reconocer nuestras historias particulares y de descubrir modos en que podemos ser una parroquia católica, viniendo de diversas culturas y etnias.

La llamada a la misión permanente

Hoy más que nunca es indispensable que las parroquias reivindiquen sus raíces y vocación misioneras. La creciente diversidad cultural en miles de parroquias en todo Estados Unidos exige que los párrocos y sus equipos salgan al encuentro de los recién llegados ahí donde se encuentran en sus vidas. En algunos casos, son los residentes católicos de muchos años

MISIÓN

en un vecindario quienes necesitan que se los visite con la Buena Noticia y se los invite a la participación activa en la vida y la misión de la comunidad parroquial. La misión de la parroquia también se extiende a los no católicos, y en especial a los más vulnerables. La obra de Caridades Católicas y otras agencias de ministerio social católico es muy importante para la misión de la Iglesia. Sin embargo, cada parroquia se beneficia al practicar las obras de misericordia directamente con las personas que viven en el vecindario. Es más, la celebración de los sacramentos, y en especial de la Eucaristía, la formación continua en la fe católica, la necesidad de nutrir la vida de oración, la llamada a construir la Iglesia como la comunidad amada y el constante ministerio de solidaridad con los más vulnerables son dimensiones esenciales de la vida cristiana. Todos los católicos bautizados que viven en una parroquia concreta necesitan acceso a la práctica de todas las dimensiones de su fe católica.

¿Cómo pueden los párrocos y sus equipos salir al encuentro de los diversos grupos culturales presentes en la parroquia? ¿Cómo pueden saber que están haciendo las cosas correctamente? ¿Cuál debería ser la meta final en acoger a estas comunidades? ¿Cómo se logra la unidad en la diversidad entre feligreses de diversas culturas y etnias? ¿Cómo se promueve una saludable interacción de los nuevos inmigrantes católicos en la vida de la Iglesia y en la sociedad de Estados Unidos? Nuestra propia historia y prácticas pastorales anteriores nos pueden ayudar a manejar estas y otras cuestiones que emergen en el contexto de las parroquias compartidas.

Las parroquias compartidas y el principio de integración/inclusión eclesial

En 1999, el beato papa Juan Pablo II escribió a las distintas iglesias culturales de Norteamérica y Latinoamérica sobre la llamada a la unidad en la diversidad en la Exhortación Apostólica *Ecclesia in America*:

> La Iglesia es signo de comunión porque sus miembros, como sarmientos, participan de la misma vida de Cristo, la verdadera vid (cf. Jn 15:5). En efecto, por la comunión con Cristo, Cabeza del Cuerpo místico, entramos en comunión viva con todos los creyentes. Esta comunión, existente en la Iglesia y esencial a su naturaleza, debe manifestarse a través de signos concretos. (no. 33)

El Santo Padre veía a los católicos de las Américas encontrando la unidad a través de un proceso de conversión espiritual, seguido de signos concretos de comunión, y de solidaridad con todos los seres humanos. Tal comunión y solidaridad también se extienden a toda cultura en la Iglesia universal, que abraza a toda la familia humana. Dicho de otro modo, nos sentimos transformados concretamente por las relaciones que tenemos unos con otros en Cristo a medida que, en Cristo, construimos la comunidad amada. Llamamos a este proceso de transformación y crecimiento en el amor *integración/inclusión eclesial*. En él, fortalecemos los vínculos de comunión en Cristo, que son animados por el Espíritu Santo y se manifiestan en el Bautismo y la Eucaristía. El principio de integración/inclusión eclesial es particularmente importante cuando tratamos de fortalecer los vínculos de comunión en Cristo entre los fieles de diversas culturas, razas y etnias, y en dar la bienvenida a los nuevos inmigrantes.

Más concretamente, el principio de integración/inclusión eclesial busca dar la bienvenida a los nuevos inmigrantes a nuestras parroquias e instituciones desarrollando ministerios orientados a culturas específicas, que afirman sus valores culturales y las tradiciones religiosas que reflejan el evangelio. Más aún, llama a un enriquecimiento mutuo a través de la interacción entre todos los grupos culturales presentes en las parroquias y en otras instituciones católicas. La integración/inclusión eclesial no se debe confundir con asimilación. Una política de asimilación espera que los nuevos inmigrantes abandonen su lengua, cultura, valores y tradiciones para poder ser aceptados como miembros de la parroquia. La historia muestra que una política de asimilación aliena a los nuevos inmigrantes católicos de la Iglesia y los hace así más vulnerables a grupos religiosos proselitistas y a la secularización. Más de doscientos años de historia católica en Estados Unidos muestran que la Iglesia está en su mejor momento cuando abraza la diversidad cultural por medio del principio de integración/inclusión eclesial. Esto es, cuando toma en consideración los valores culturales, las tradiciones y las expresiones de fe de los nuevos inmigrantes como parte integral de su ser.

Integración/inclusión eclesial en Estados Unidos

El principio de la integración/inclusión eclesial fue el fundamento del *modelo de parroquia nacional*. Las parroquias nacionales fueron diseñadas como respuesta pastoral para proporcionar a los nuevos inmigrantes católicos europeos el espacio eclesial que necesitaban para vivir su fe, orar y dar culto en el contexto de su propia cultura, idioma y tradiciones. Las parroquias nacionales tuvieron mucho éxito en ayudar a los nuevos inmigrantes y a sus hijos a fortalecer su identidad católica mientras se adaptaban a la vida en Estados Unidos con el correr del tiempo. Una gran parte del sistema de escuelas católicas de Estados Unidos surgió de las parroquias nacionales como modo de asegurarse de que las futuras generaciones heredarían la fe católica.

El éxito del *modelo de parroquia nacional* en dar la bienvenida a los inmigrantes católicos de Europa a través de un proceso de integración/inclusión eclesial es una de las más importantes razones por las que tenemos más de setenta millones de católicos que viven en Estados Unidos hoy día. El éxito de la Iglesia entre los católicos afroamericanos y los nativos americanos de más de dos siglos también se ha apoyado en la medida a la que la Iglesia fue capaz de encarnar los valores evangélicos en el corazón de esas culturas.

Los años que siguieron a la Segunda Guerra Mundial vieron el *modelo de parroquia nacional* desvanecerse debido al fin de la inmigración masiva de Europa. Unos cuantos años más tarde, el fin de la segregación y la ola masiva de inmigrantes del hemisferio sur contribuyeron a la diversidad cultural que experimentamos hoy en nuestros barrios y parroquias. Estos factores históricos, combinados con el número limitado de sacerdotes y la escasez de recursos económicos, constituyen el contexto en el que emerge la parroquia compartida como respuesta pastoral que da nueva vida a la Iglesia hoy.

El principio de integración/inclusión eclesial que dio tanto éxito al *modelo de parroquia nacional*, también está en el núcleo del *modelo de parroquia compartida*. La diferencia entre los dos modelos es que cada parroquia nacional servía a los católicos de un país europeo concreto, normalmente bajo el liderazgo de un sacerdote de ese país y en un momento histórico en que la Iglesia Católica estaba creciendo significativamente, mientras que una parroquia compartida sirve a personas de diferentes culturas y etnias que comparten un párroco, los edificios, los horarios y otros recursos. A menudo estas parroquias son encargadas al liderazgo de un párroco que es un nuevo inmigrante. Tal compartir de espacio y recursos puede ser muy desafiante en ocasiones, pero también hace espacio a la gracia de Dios para modelar la comunidad amada que nos llama a ser.

El modelo de unidad en la diversidad en las Escrituras

Las Escrituras y la tradición cristiana inspiran y guían a la Iglesia en su comprensión y construcción de la unidad eclesial en medio de la diversidad humana. En el Antiguo Testamento, Isaías predica sobre Dios que congrega no solo a Israel, sino a todas las naciones a su santa montaña en paz (Is 2:2–4). En el Nuevo Testamento, escuchamos a san Pedro proclamar que "Dios no hace distinción de personas" cuando relata cómo el Espíritu Santo ha

UNIDAD EN LA DIVERSIDAD

escogido a los gentiles, gente de una cultura totalmente distinta, para ser bautizados sin necesitar abrazar las costumbres judías (Hch 10). La imagen de un solo cuerpo es quizá la expresión más significativa de honrar la diversidad mientras que se afirma la unidad de un cuerpo en Cristo. San Pablo hablaba a la iglesia en Corinto sobre la diversidad de dones espirituales y cómo todos esos dones encuentran su fuente y origen en el Espíritu Santo. Tal diversidad está centrada en los miembros del cuerpo, enfatizando sus identidades culturales concretas o su estilo de vida. "Porque todos nosotros, seamos judíos o no judíos, esclavos o libres, hemos sido bautizados en un mismo Espíritu, para formar un solo cuerpo, y a todos se nos ha dado a beber del mismo Espíritu" (1 Cor 12:13). Este énfasis en abrazar la diversidad humana, particularmente en referencia a los judíos y los griegos, se encuentra en todas las cartas de Pablo. En la carta a los Gálatas, Pablo enseña que "ya no existe diferencia entre judíos y no judíos, entre esclavos y libres, entre varón y mujer, porque todos ustedes son uno en Cristo Jesús" (Gal 3:28). Una declaración parecida se encuentra en la carta a los Romanos: "Porque no existe diferencia entre judío y no judío, ya que uno mismo es el Señor de todos, espléndido con todos los que lo invocan, pues 'todo el que invoque al Señor como a su Dios, será salvado por él'" (Rom 10:12–13). San Pablo pide que todos los líderes cristianos sean todo para todos (cf. 1 Cor 9:22), y enfáticamente insiste en un evangelio que no exija a los gentiles que se conviertan en judíos, porque en Cristo "ya no existe diferencia entre judíos y no judíos" (Gal 3:28).

La historia cristiana más famosa sobre la unidad en la diversidad es la de Pentecostés, en Hechos de los Apóstoles, que a veces se nombra como "el nacimiento de la Iglesia". En el segundo capítulo de Hechos, el Espíritu Santo viene en forma de viento fuerte y llamas de fuego que se posan sobre las cabezas de los discípulos congregados en el Cenáculo. Inmediatamente empiezan a anunciar la Buena Noticia de Jesucristo a la multitud de orígenes culturales diversos que se había congregado cerca para la fiesta judía de Pentecostés. Todos los Apóstoles estaban hablando en su propio idioma arameo, pero cada persona presente los oía en su propia lengua. Así, la gente retiene su propia lengua y cultura, pero son capaces de compartir la Buena Noticia.

El capítulo 15 de Hechos también habla de la igualdad de judíos y gentiles en Cristo. La declaración viene de Pedro, pero responde a la inclusión que Pablo había predicado al igualar a judíos y gentiles ante Cristo y ante Dios. "Hermanos: Ustedes saben que, ya desde los primeros días, Dios me eligió entre ustedes para que los paganos oyeran, por mi medio, las palabras del Evangelio y creyeran. Dios, que conoce los corazones, mostró su aprobación dándoles el Espírito Santo, igual que a nosotros. No hizo distinción alguna, ya que purificó sus corazones con la fe." (Hch 15:7–9).

El ejemplo de Hechos 6:1–7 también es pertinente aquí como modelo de unidad en la diversidad. En esta historia, los diáconos fueron elegidos porque las viudas de los helenistas estaban siendo abandonadas. El asunto era de idioma y por tanto de nacionalidad y cultura, y la meta era la inclusión.

Las Escrituras y la tradición cristiana son bastante consistentes en proclamar el evangelio a todas las naciones y culturas. También son claras en presentar un modelo de ministros capaces y dispuestos a ser todo para todos (cf. 1 Cor 9:22). Tal modelo de ministerio es particularmente necesario en parroquias compartidas, en que las los pastores podrían sentirse presionados en distintas direcciones por los fieles. El ministerio del párroco es esencial en moldear la comunidad amada en su parroquia. Todos los párrocos que participaron en la consulta estuvieron de acuerdo en que el factor más importante para lograr un alto grado de integración/inclusión eclesial en parroquias compartidas es un párroco que ha abrazado a todos los feligreses de diversas culturas como los suyos. Tanto si el párroco nació en Estados Unidos como si nació en el extranjero, y sin importar de qué grupo racial o cultural proviene, el párroco es el signo primordial de unidad y de amor pastoral en la parroquia, junto con el obispo diocesano. Es muy improbable que una parroquia compartida adquiera un alto nivel de integración/inclusión eclesial si el párroco no es ejemplo de tal solicitud pastoral hacia todos sus feligreses.

El ministerio y la espiritualidad del párroco

En su propio núcleo, la Iglesia Católica es una comunidad eucarística. Es en la celebración de la liturgia dominical donde los católicos se acercan más íntimamente a Cristo como discípulos y como miembros de su Iglesia. Cristo nos dejó el don de sí mismo en la Eucaristía, que se actualiza en el ministerio litúrgico de los Apóstoles y sus sucesores. A medida que el número de los bautizados crecía a lo largo del tiempo, los obispos ordenaron a sacerdotes como extensión de su ministerio apostólico para que toda persona bautizada pudiera compartir en el sacramento de la Eucaristía y en toda la vida y misión de la Iglesia. Cuando un sacerdote es nombrado párroco por su obispo, ese sacerdote se hace responsable del bienestar de todo el pueblo que vive dentro de los límites parroquiales. Como párroco, el sacerdote se convierte en símbolo de unidad para los fieles confiados a su cuidado, no solo *in persona Christi* durante la celebración de la Eucaristía, sino también como una persona que es intermediaria del amor de Dios para todos, sin importar las diferencias culturales, raciales o étnicas. El personal y los líderes parroquiales siguen al liderazgo de su párroco para encontrar modos eficaces de servir en comunidades culturalmente diversas, en un espíritu de unidad en la diversidad.

La espiritualidad que describe Juan Pablo II en *Ecclesia in America* habla con elocuencia sobre la espiritualidad que sostiene al párroco y su ministerio. Tal espiritualidad tiene un carácter misionero que busca constantemente un encuentro con el Jesucristo vivo como camino a la conversión, la comunión y la solidaridad. El personal parroquial y los líderes que sirven a poblaciones diversas también se sienten inspirados y movidos por el Espíritu Santo a crear un ambiente de intimidad espiritual en el cual los feligreses de distintos orígenes culturales y etnias pueden experimentar un encuentro personal con Cristo, lo que los lleva a la conversión, la comunión y la solidaridad de unos con otros.

Las siguientes reflexiones se basan en los comentarios compartidos por los párrocos que participaron en la consulta. Tienen aplicación no solo a ellos mismos como párrocos, sino a su personal y a los líderes principales de la parroquia. El consenso de los párrocos indicaba que la mejor manera de saber si se está siendo eficaz en acercar a las personas más a Cristo es cuando uno mismo se siente más cerca de Cristo al entrar en relación con ellas.

Encuentro: Los párrocos y sus equipos están dispuestos y son capaces de relacionarse a nivel personal con feligreses de distintas culturas y orígenes. Sentirse bienvenidos y cómodos unos con otros es clave para experimentar el amor de Dios, tanto, si es en la liturgia, el aula de clases, eventos sociales, trabajando en obras de misericordia, en eventos familiares significativos o respondiendo a quien pide ayuda. Ciertamente somos la voz, los brazos, los pies y el amor de Cristo cuando nos relacionamos con otros como ministros del Cuerpo de Cristo.

Conversión: Nuestros corazones y mentes se transforman constantemente a medida que experimentamos la gracia de Dios en nuestras vidas y la compartimos con los demás. Celebrar la liturgia dominical con una comunidad cultural distinta a la propia, escuchar las historias de personas diferentes a uno mismo, disfrutar la hospitalidad de una familia inmigrante que comparte contigo desde su propia pobreza, visitar a las personas en un hospital o en prisión, ver la generosidad de feligreses ya asentados hacia las nuevas

ESPIRITUALIDAD PARA LA INTEGRACIÓN/INCLUSIÓN ECLESIAL

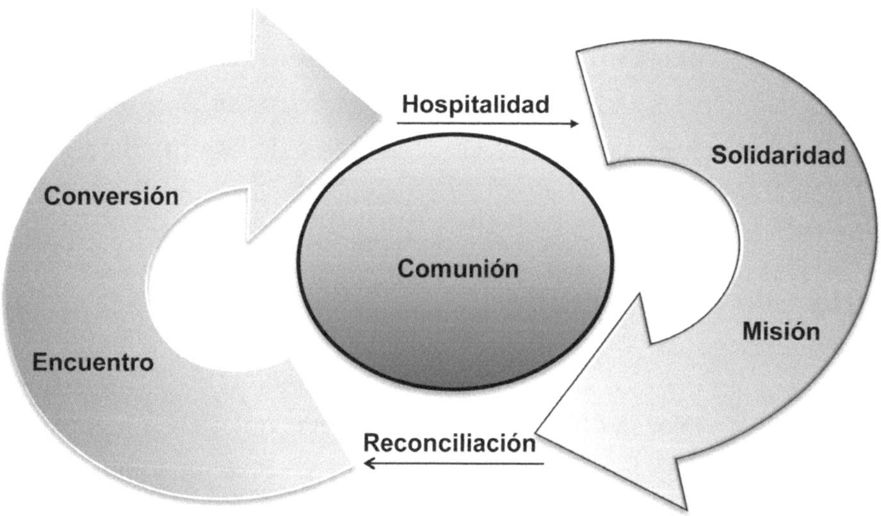

familias inmigrantes, dar testimonio de la inquebrantable fe en el amor de Dios de quienes viven en la pobreza en tu propia parroquia . . . todas estas experiencias conducen a los párrocos y a sus equipos a decir: "ellos hicieron más por mí que lo que yo hice por ellos".

Comunión: Muchas parroquias compartidas experimentan un sentido de comunidad durante liturgias bilingües o multiculturales que están bien planificadas y celebradas en armonía —en picnics parroquiales y otros eventos sociales en los que todos los feligreses comparten comida, música, arte y servicio y en que los miembros culturalmente diversos de la parroquia trabajan juntos— en servicios sociales como el ministerio de san Vicente de Paúl, en campañas sociales, en pintar el edificio de la parroquia, reunirse para una procesión el Viernes Santo, participar en grupos de oración, tomar decisiones como miembros del consejo parroquial, administrar los recursos como miembros del consejo económico, organizar actividades de recaudación de fondos, servirse mutuamente como miembros del personal parroquial y aprender juntos durante sesiones de formación sobre la misión y función del consejo parroquial.

Solidaridad: Apoyar una reforma justa y humanitaria del sistema migratorio bajo los principios de la Doctrina Social de la Iglesia, salir al encuentro de los ancianos y enfermos, apoyar activamente ministerios que sirven a madres solteras y familias rotas, promover una cultura de vida y la dignidad de la persona humana desde la concepción a la muerte natural, ayudar a familias a lograr metas educativas más altas, particularmente a los jóvenes de familias inmigrantes nuevas, y desarrollar una relación de hermandad con otra parroquia en la diócesis o en otro país, todos estos son ejemplos de cómo se vive la solidaridad en una parroquia intercultural.

Según los párrocos que participaron en la consulta, dos de las dimensiones espirituales más importantes en parroquias compartidas son la hospitalidad y la reconciliación. Estos dos catalizadores bíblicos de la vida cristiana son como los goznes del ministerio en familias compartidas y, de hecho, en cualquier familia, parroquia o institución católica.

Hospitalidad: En el contexto de parroquias compartidas estamos llamados a darnos la bienvenida unos a otros, particularmente al forastero entre nosotros. La hospitalidad no es una acción aislada o gesto de dar la bienvenida a otros. Tener hospitalidad es decirle a la otra persona "aquí hay espacio para ti". En la Escritura, la hospitalidad es un valor y un principio; es una manera de estar en el mundo con Dios y unos con otros. Dios es el anfitrión generoso. Dios nos congrega alrededor de su mesa. Es Jesús quien lava los pies de sus discípulos y prepara el desayuno a sus discípulos a orillas del lago. Dios nos da ejemplo de una hospitalidad transformadora con pasión por el servicio a los demás, y en especial a los más necesitados. En el sentido bíblico, una parroquia acogedora es la que sabe cómo dar la bienvenida a otros y lo hace porque es a lo que nos llama el Evangelio. Es a lo que nos llama la Iglesia. El gran mandato de hacer discípulos de todas las naciones implica dar la bienvenida a personas de todas las naciones, para que puedan saber que somos cristianos por el modo en que nos amamos unos a otros. El profeta Isaías habla de esta llamada a la hospitalidad:

> *Los haré en medio de mi pueblo más célebres y poderosos, que si tuvieran hijos e hijas. Los haré eternamente famosos, y nunca serán olvidados. . . . pues me casa será llamada casa de oración para todos los pueblos. (Biblia de América, Is 56:5–7)*

Los párrocos que participaron en la consulta para la elaboración de esta guía son expertos en el hacer que personas de distintas culturas y etnias se sientan bienvenidas en la casa de Dios. Tal actitud de bienvenida también está presente en su personal y liderazgo parroquial, ya que ven en

HOSPITALIDAD

todos los fieles la herencia que Dios ha encomendado a su cuidado. El Dr. Timothy Matovina habla de "venir a casa" como el tipo de hospitalidad que las parroquias deben extender a los recién llegados. El venir a casa acoge a los inmigrantes católicos no como huéspedes, sino como miembros plenos de la Iglesia Católica en virtud de su Bautismo. En la Escritura, la misión y la hospitalidad están entrelazadas. Dios nos busca y nos acoge siempre, como Pastor amoroso. Estamos llamados a hacer lo mismo unos con otros, para que todos los católicos se sientan en casa.

Así como una sonrisa acogedora puede ser el principio de una amistad, una parroquia acogedora busca hacer que la gente se sienta en casa y desarrolle un sentido de pertenencia a la comunidad de fe. Un sentido de pertenencia puede a su vez convertirse en un sentido de posesión, cuando los recién llegados plenamente abrazan su llamada al discipulado como miembros de una parroquia concreta. Es importante darse cuenta de que una espiritualidad de hospitalidad transforma no solo a quienes dan la bienvenida, sino también a quienes están siendo recibidos. Dar la bienvenida al forastero significa amar al forastero. De alguna manera, todos somos forasteros hasta que llegamos a conocernos unos a otros y nos relacionamos en el amor de Dios por nosotros.

Reconciliación: Junto con la hospitalidad, la reconciliación es otro motor que mueve el proceso de integración/inclusión eclesial. Los párrocos que participaron en la consulta pusieron mucho énfasis en la importancia de escuchar profundamente las preocupaciones que a menudo surgen sobre los recién llegados por parte de los feligreses más veteranos. Los cambios demográficos en ciudades y vecindarios pueden resultar preocupantes para los residentes más antiguos que están acostumbrados a un cierto modo de hacer las cosas: escuchar cierto idioma, ver rostros familiares e interactuar con personas a quienes conocen. El cambio es particularmente desafiante cuando los feligreses antiguos de una comunidad culturalmente homogénea se enteran de que deben dar la bienvenida a los nuevos inmigrantes católicos de distintos orígenes culturales y étnicos, como miembros de la parroquia. La perspectiva de compartir las dependencias y recursos de la parroquia con personas a las que no conocen puede generar un sentido de pérdida de su propio espacio y un temor a que los recién llegados no cuiden tan bien de las cosas, o incluso de que se apoderen de la parroquia que ha sido una parte tan importante de sus vidas. Expresiones como *mis abuelos construyeron esta parroquia,* o *fue tan difícil para nosotros tener por fin una parroquia que pudiéramos sentir como nuestra y ahora* *los recién llegados quizá la tomen como suya* expresan sentimientos de incertidumbre, pérdida e incluso duelo, que son muy reales y tienen que tener tomarse en serio. Estas experiencias a menudo llevan a muchos en la comunidad receptora a tomar el papel de *anfitrión dudoso*.

Pero igualmente importante es la necesidad de estar atentos a las luchas y experiencias traumáticas que pueden traer a los recién llegados a nuestras ciudades y vecindarios. La mayoría de los inmigrantes se vieron forzados a dejar su hogar y sus familias a causa de la pobreza, la violencia o la persecución y ahora viven en un país distinto con una cultura y un idioma distintos. Para quienes son católicos, en muchos casos la Iglesia Católica, y en particular la parroquia, es el lugar donde pueden buscar un cierto grado de seguridad y confianza, un "hogar lejos del hogar". A menudo, sin embargo, encuentran estructuras que quizá no funcionen en los modos familiares de las parroquias católicas a las que estaban acostumbrados en sus países. Podrían sentirse ignorados, experimentar rechazo e incluso sufrir discriminación en su nuevo ambiente. Frecuentemente estas experiencias pueden también hacerlos sentirse o actuar como *huéspedes renuentes*.

Unir estas dos realidades del *anfitrión dudoso* y el *huésped renuente* requiere un verdadero ministerio de reconciliación que construya un puente entre los feligreses bien establecidos y los recién llegados. Tal ministerio de reconciliación solo puede estar inspirado por el Espíritu Santo y modelado por Cristo. Las Escrituras y nuestra tradición católica son testigos vivos de la obra del Espíritu, construyendo un puente entre ricos y pobres, judíos y gentiles, caseros y forasteros. Depende de cada generación y cada parroquia concreta continuar este ministerio de reconciliación como el modo de construir la comunidad amada en las parroquias compartidas y en nuestras instituciones católicas. Escuchar profundamente las preocupaciones y temores, tanto de los feligreses veteranos como de los recién llegados, y acompañarlos en su duelo por la pérdida de lo que les era familiar, está en el núcleo del ministerio de reconciliación en parroquias compartidas.

PARTE III

El proceso de desarrollo de integración/inclusión eclesial y corresponsabilidad en parroquias compartidas

Los nueve movimientos de integración/inclusión eclesial

La tercera parte de esta guía se centra en cómo se logra, de hecho, la integración/inclusión eclesial en las parroquias compartidas. Los párrocos que participaron en la consulta estuvieron de acuerdo en que la integración/inclusión eclesial es un proceso de desarrollo que tiene lugar a lo largo del tiempo y que es guiado por el amor unificador del Espíritu Santo. Los párrocos afirmaron que sigue un proceso que lleva a la gente de la *bienvenida* a *pertenecer* y a la *corresponsabilidad*. Los párrocos también enfatizaron que cuanto más alto es el nivel de integración/inclusión eclesial, más alto es el nivel de corresponsabilidad en parroquias compartidas.

Los objetivos de *bienvenida, pertenencia* y *corresponsabilidad* hacen eco a las metas de ministerio en situaciones multiculturales del P. Robert Schreiter. *La bienvenida* se relaciona con la meta de *reconocimiento del otro como diferente*. Implica reconocer su presencia y mostrar hospitalidad en un modo que el otro pueda entender. *Pertenecer* se relaciona con la meta de *respetar las diferencias culturales* y describe cómo se forman las relaciones a través de fronteras culturales. *Corresponsabilidad* se relaciona con la meta de *sana interacción,*

DE RECIÉN LLEGADOS A CORRESPONSABLES EN LA COMUNIDAD DE FE

descrita como un tipo de comunión en el que ninguno de los grupos pierde su propia identidad pero ha tomado para sí elementos del otro grupo. Hay un sentido de posesión compartida y confianza que permite una interacción generosa mutual. El aspecto de desarrollo de este proceso también se basa en un enfoque de sentido común: la bienvenida conduce a un sentido de pertenencia, lo cual a su vez lleva a un sentido de posesión y de relaciones interculturales más sanas.

A fin de proporcionar un mapa de ruta para alcanzar los objetivos de *bienvenida, pertenencia* y *corresponsabilidad*, esta guía presenta nueve movimientos o indicadores que describen cómo se logra de hecho la integración/inclusión eclesial. Es importante darse cuenta de que los nueve movimientos no describen un programa o método rígido. Más bien, los nueve movimientos ilustran un proceso dinámico de *bienvenida, pertenencia* y *corresponsabilidad* que implica el acompañamiento pastoral de los fieles por parte del párroco y su equipo. Este proceso pastoral se hace eco de las palabras que expresó el papa Francisco en su primera homilía como papa:

> Quisiera que todos, después de estos días de gracia, tengamos el valor, precisamente el valor, de caminar en presencia del Señor, con la cruz del Señor; de edificar la Iglesia sobre la sangre del Señor, derramada en la cruz; y de confesar la única gloria: Cristo crucificado. Y así la Iglesia avanzará. (Papa Francisco, Homilía, 14 de marzo de 2013)

El proceso dinámico de integración/inclusión eclesial nos llama al proceso continuo de caminar con los fieles confiados a nuestro cuidado, construyendo la comunidad amada entre ellos y profesando la Muerte y

PROCESO PARA LA INTEGRACIÓN/INCLUSIÓN ECLESIAL

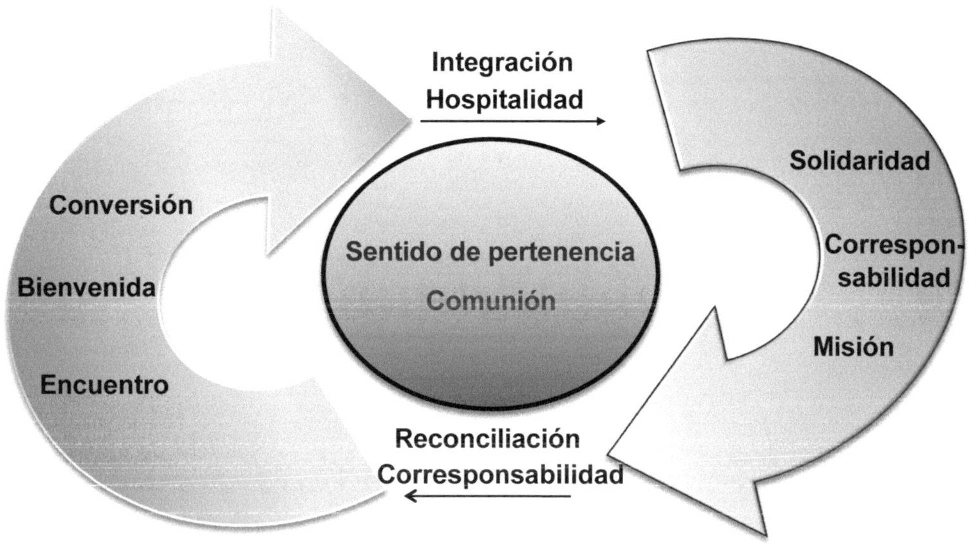

Resurrección de Cristo como razón principal de nuestra esperanza y nuestra misión.

El siguiente ejemplo despliega los nueve movimientos de integración/inclusión eclesial en el contexto de una parroquia compartida. El ejemplo presenta una parroquia a la que han llegado recientemente un buen número de familias vietnamitas e hispanas. La triple meta del párroco y su equipo es lograr un alto nivel de *bienvenida*, *pertenencia* y *corresponsabilidad* entre los grupos católicos culturalmente diversos que viven dentro de los límites de la parroquia. Además de funcionar como mapa de ruta, los objetivos se pueden usar también para evaluar el nivel de corresponsabilidad entre los nuevos inmigrantes, que crece en proporción directa al nivel de integración/inclusión eclesial logrado.

El ejemplo utiliza la estructura básica presente en muchas parroquias —párroco, personal, consejo parroquial y consejo de finanzas— para ilustrar cómo esta estructura varía a medida que avanza el proceso de integración/inclusión eclesial. Enfatiza el tipo de estilo de liderazgo más necesario del párroco para hacer avanzar el proceso. El ejemplo también incluye tres momentos de crisis a los que las parroquias compartidas se enfrentan a menudo. La primera crisis tiene que ver con la resistencia al cambio; la segunda, con la resistencia a compartir; y la tercera con la resistencia a la posesión mutua.

Bienvenida

Movimiento 1: Misión

Después de darse cuenta de la presencia significativa de los católicos vietnamitas e hispanos que viven dentro de los límites de la parroquia, el párroco toma la decisión de salir a su encuentro. Se organiza un grupo

MOVIMIENTO 1—MISIÓN

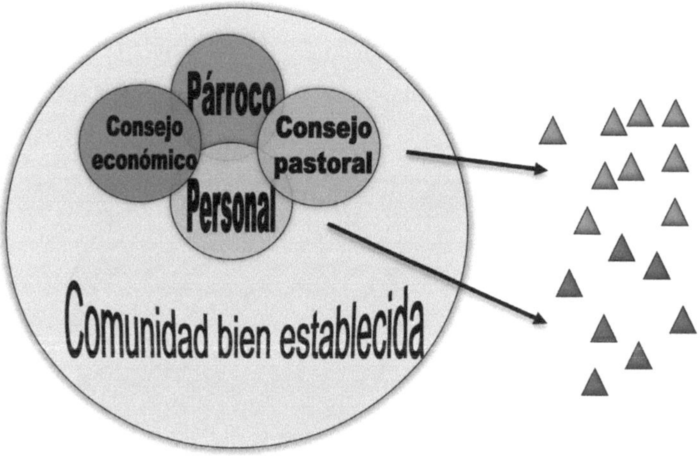

Territorio parroquial

de líderes parroquiales para llevar a cabo un censo en áreas donde vive un buen número de familias vietnamitas e hispanas. El censo se lleva a cabo en el espíritu de misión, llevando saludos del párroco a las personas a quienes se visita, junto con una invitación a tomar parte en la vida y la misión de la parroquia como su hogar. El estilo de liderazgo del párroco es proactivo, con un énfasis en la misión de alcanzar a todas las personas que residen dentro de los límites parroquiales.

Movimiento 2: Llegar a casa

Unas cuantas familias vietnamitas e hispanas responden inmediatamente a la invitación del párroco y empiezan a asistir a la liturgia dominical en inglés. La inmensa mayoría, sin embargo, no se siente cómoda participando en la Misa o en otras actividades parroquiales en inglés o con personas a las que no conocen. Al darse cuenta de la importancia del idioma, la cultura y las tradiciones religiosas de los nuevos inmigrantes católicos, el párroco decide crear un *espacio eclesial* para los vietnamitas e hispanos en su parroquia proporcionando ministerios culturalmente específicos para estas nuevas comunidades. Crear un *espacio eclesial* comienza por establecer la liturgia dominical en vietnamita y español. Tal decisión es el signo *par excellence* de que los vietnamitas y los hispanos, en este caso, han sido acogidos no solo como individuos sino como comunidades con necesidades y aspiraciones específicas como católicos bautizados. La decisión que toma el párroco de establecer la Misa en idiomas distintos al inglés a menudo lleva a la *crisis*. El personal y otros líderes parroquiales podrían sentirse preocupados por las consecuencias que podría tener este cambio. Es común pensar que tener la Misa en distintos idiomas podría dividir a la parroquia. Sin embargo, el párroco sabe que la parroquia ya está dividida entre los católicos bautizados que ya están congregados y los que están esparcidos.

La experiencia en más de siete mil parroquias en todo Estados Unidos muestra que ofrecer la liturgia dominical en el idioma y

MOVIMIENTO 2—LLEGAR A CASA: HACER QUE LA GENTE SE SIENTA EN CASA

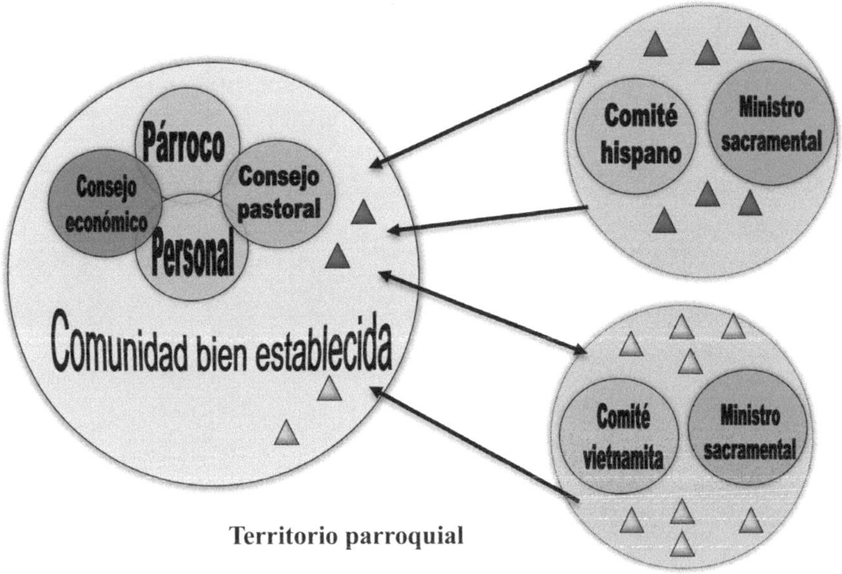

contexto cultural de los nuevos inmigrantes católicos crea las condiciones iniciales para la interacción y la unidad. Proporciona a los nuevos inmigrantes el espacio eclesial que necesitan para fortalecer su identidad católica y adaptarse a vivir en Estados Unidos desde una posición de fortaleza. Les da también una oportunidad de desarrollar una capacidad ministerial, comenzando por los ministerios litúrgicos y la formación de un equipo de liderazgo para coordinar los ministerios. El establecimiento de la liturgia dominical, en vietnamita o en español, a menudo requiere la ayuda de sacerdotes que puedan celebrar la Misa en esos idiomas, mientras el párroco desarrolla la capacidad de hacerlo él mismo. Sin embargo, *la claridad eclesial* es esencial para reconocer que la responsabilidad pastoral por todos los feligreses reside en el párroco. Una comprensión clara por parte del ministro sacramental de que él está ayudando al párroco en su ministerio y no apoderándose como "párroco *de facto*" de la comunidad vietnamita o hispana, ha demostrado ser extremadamente útil para evitar la confusión y el conflicto potencial. Establecer la liturgia dominical en vietnamita o español es un paso necesario hacia el logro de la unidad en la diversidad en el futuro. La práctica de corresponsabilidad toma lugar en forma de tiempo y talento que ofrecen los recién llegados, particularmente dentro de sus comunidades respectivas. Compartir los recursos económicos a menudo está muy limitado en este momento.

Movimiento 3: Crecimiento ministerial

Una vez que se ha establecido la liturgia dominical, tanto la comunidad vietnamita como la hispana comienzan a desarrollar ministerios y ministros. En primer lugar se desarrollan los ministerios litúrgicos, luego comienza la formación catequética para la recepción de los sacramentos. A esto le siguen otros ministerios en las áreas de la oración, los servicios sociales, el ministerio juvenil, la construcción

MOVIMIENTO 3—CRECIMIENTO MINISTERIAL: ORGANIZAR Y DESARROLLAR MINISTERIOS Y MINISTROS

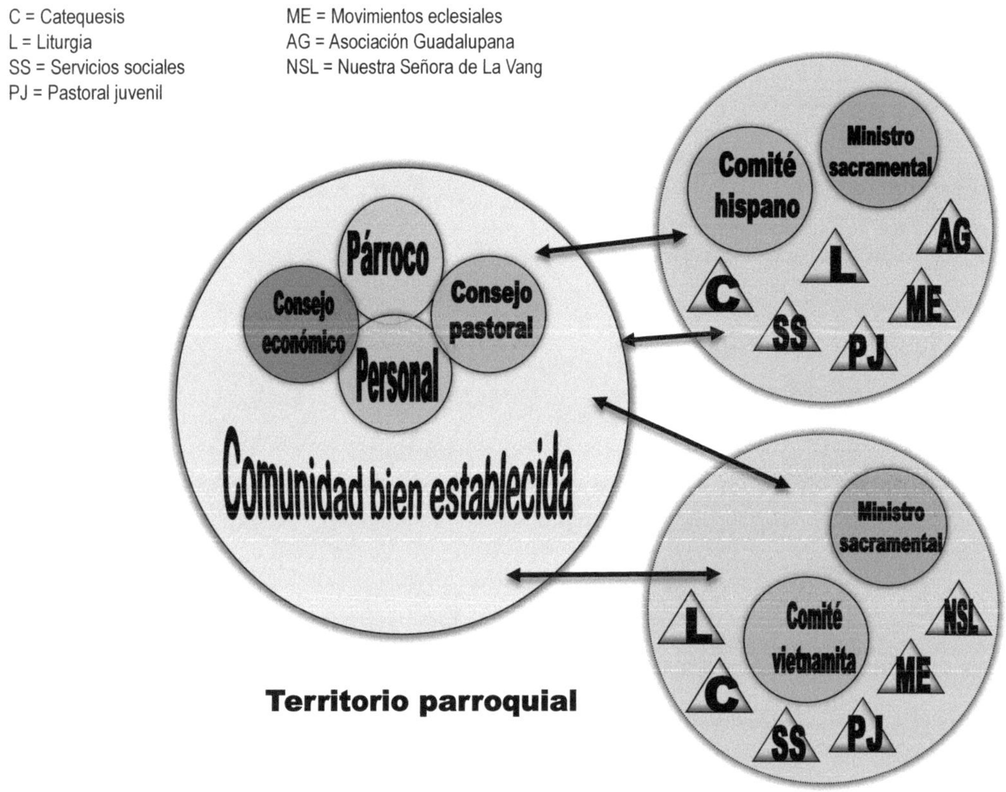

de la comunidad, la corresponsabilidad y otros. En algunos casos, en especial en la comunidad latina, este proceso se apoya en el establecimiento y la fuerte presencia de movimientos eclesiales laicos y pequeñas comunidades eclesiales. El desarrollo exitoso de los ministerios lleva a un aumento en el tamaño y mayor participación de las nuevas comunidades, y a su necesidad de más recursos.

El crecimiento resulta en una *segunda crisis* que reclama un cambio en el modo en que se usan los recursos y que a menudo se expresa por medio de quejas. Por una parte, los recién llegados desarrollan un sentido de pertenencia a la parroquia que les permite esperar que vengan más recursos, tales como un mejor horario para su liturgia dominical, el uso de un nuevo espacio, un programa catequético que permita a los padres enseñar la fe a sus propios hijos, la celebración de las tradiciones propias de su cultura, etc. Por otra parte, los feligreses veteranos empiezan a quejarse sobre las exigencias constantes de los recién llegados a más acceso en términos de tiempo, espacio y programas, o de que los párrocos pasan demasiado tiempo con ellos. Escuchar las quejas de la gente no es muy agradable. Sin embargo, es un signo de que los recién llegados han logrado un gran nivel de pertenencia a la parroquia. También indica la necesidad de enfocarse en construir relaciones a través de las culturas para que la gente pueda pasar de un lenguaje de "nosotros-ellos" a otro de "nosotros".

No es poco frecuente que las parroquias compartidas se atasquen en este movimiento cuando las personas de las distintas comunidades hacen grandes esfuerzos para "tolerarse" mutuamente y evitar el conflicto. Este tipo de tolerancia del otro no es suficiente para continuar en el camino hacia una interacción sana entre los distintos grupos culturales de la parroquia. Solamente cuando las personas están dispuestas a desarrollar relaciones entre las culturas y ministerios puede la comunidad parroquial, en su totalidad, avanzar en el camino hacia la integración/inclusión eclesial. El estilo de liderazgo del párroco en este momento reclama buenas destrezas de escucha y crea un ambiente de seguridad y confianza en que los líderes de las distintas comunidades pueden compartir sus preocupaciones y comenzar un proceso de diálogo intercultural y entendimiento mutuo. El nivel de corresponsabilidad aumenta significativamente en términos de tiempo y talento. Los recursos económicos también pueden ser significativos, dependiendo de la libertad que tengan las comunidades vietnamitas e hispanas de desarrollar ministerios y ministros y de practicar formas de recaudación de fondos que sean relevantes para cada comunidad. La ofrenda en la Misa podría ser limitada todavía, ya que las prácticas como usar los sobres o comprometerse a una cantidad fija semanalmente podrían resultarles extrañas.

Pertenecer

Movimiento 4: Construir relaciones entre distintas culturas

Este movimiento quizá sea el más difícil de lograr. Una de las razones es que requiere que los líderes de las diferentes comunidades culturales vayan más allá de sus propias fronteras culturales para encontrarse y conocerse mutuamente a nivel más personal. Compartir historias y perspectivas y tener experiencias comunes lleva al desarrollo de las relaciones interpersonales que mueven a las personas del lenguaje de "nosotros-ellos" al de "nosotros". La celebración de liturgias multiculturales en días de fiesta clave, los picnics anuales en que la comunidad entera se une para comer y divertirse, los festivales anuales planificados y llevados a cabo con la participación de diversos grupos y organizaciones y los retiros que se enfocan en compartir y escuchar las historias de unos y otros en el contexto de las Escrituras, entre otras cosas, son modos eficaces de construir relaciones y un mejor sentido de comunidad.

El consenso entre los párrocos que participaron en la consulta era que el amor del párroco hacia los feligreses de todos los grupos culturales puede que sea el indicador más importante, o al menos uno de los más importantes, de que una parroquia compartida ha llegado al cuarto movimiento en el proceso de integración/inclusión eclesial. Tal amor pastoral se refleja en el hecho de que el párroco conoce al liderazgo de las distintas comunidades a nivel personal y que está presente activa y regularmente en las celebraciones litúrgicas y sociales de las diversas comunidades culturales. Todos los fieles confían en el párroco, y él da ejemplo de unidad en la diversidad a su personal y equipos de líderes, convirtiéndose así en un símbolo de unidad para todos. En este estadio del proceso de integración, el ministro sacramental visitante normalmente ya no es necesario, puesto que

MOVIMIENTO 4—CONSTRUIR RELACIONES ENTRE DISTINTAS CULTURAS Y MINISTERIOS

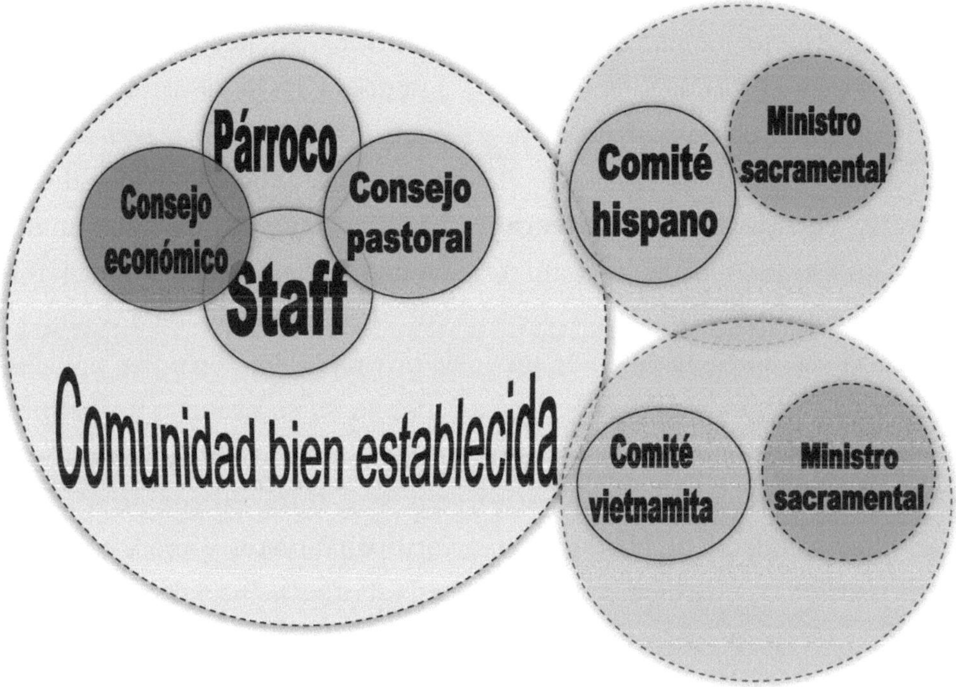

Territorio parroquial

el párroco y/o el vicario parroquial es capaz de presidir la liturgia dominical en inglés, vietnamita y español. (Sin embargo, las realidades pastorales podrían requerir otra cosa). El tiempo y el talento continúan creciendo a ritmo rápido a medida que las comunidades se agrandan. La cuestión de la contribución semanal podría surgir como un asunto difícil a medida que las diversas comunidades en la parroquia se van conociendo mejor. Este movimiento también presenta una buena oportunidad para explorar modos creativos de recaudación de fondos.

Movimiento 5: Desarrollo y formación de un liderazgo intercultural

Este movimiento enfatiza la necesidad de acompañar y formar a los líderes parroquiales para que sean competentes interculturalmente. Los miembros del consejo parroquial y el consejo económico y el personal parroquial son conscientes de las diferencias culturales presentes en la parroquia y saben cómo comunicar, trabajar y relacionarse cruzando los límites culturales. Existe el compromiso con el desarrollo continuo de la capacidad intercultural en forma de actitudes, conocimiento y destrezas que sirven mejor a una parroquia culturalmente diversa. El desarrollo continuo de la capacidad intercultural requiere el apoyo económico del personal y los líderes parroquiales para participar en talleres, sesiones de formación, clases y seminarios que ayudan a los líderes a lograr un alto nivel de capacidad intercultural. El desarrollo general ministerial de líderes de

MOVEMENT 5—CHAMPION LEADERSHIP DEVELOPMENT AND FORMATION

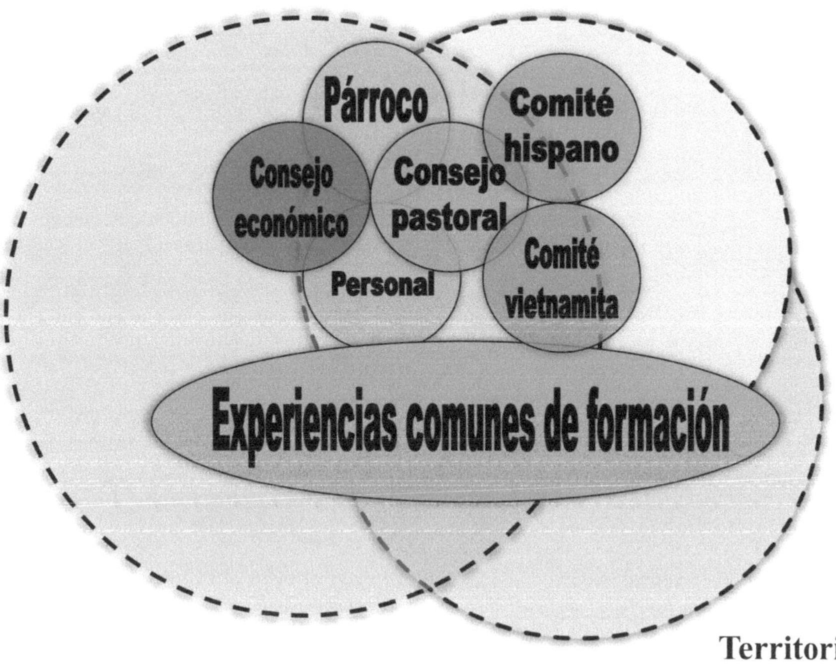

la comunidad vietnamita e hispana también es esencial para poder convertirse en personas fácilmente contratables como personal parroquial en el futuro. El párroco es mentor y entrenador para el liderazgo emergente entre las diversas comunidades a medida que se hacen más competentes interculturalmente. La corresponsabilidad se convierte en material de estudio y de desarrollo de destrezas a medida que las diversas comunidades culturales y étnicas aprenden unas de otras y colaboran más íntimamente. También prepara al liderazgo parroquial a ser más inclusivo en el proceso de toma de decisiones.

Movimiento 6: Proceso de toma de decisiones

Este movimiento desata la *tercera crisis* más común: pasar de una dinámica de ser *anfitriones-huéspedes* a un sentido de posesión común. Una parroquia compartida que ha alcanzado este nivel de inclusión/integración eclesial presenta una imagen en la que los miembros de las distintas comunidades culturales tienen un lugar en la mesa en donde se toman las decisiones, ya sea el consejo parroquial, el consejo económico o incluso el personal parroquial. El movimiento subraya el deseo de los líderes de las comunidades vietnamita e hispana de trabajar por el bienestar de toda la parroquia y no solo de los miembros de su grupo cultural concreto. Al mismo tiempo, el liderazgo de la comunidad veterana está preparado para abrazar a los nuevos líderes como coanfitriones y socios al mismo nivel.

En este punto del desarrollo, la estructura y el liderazgo de la comunidad parroquial es

MOVIMIENTO 6—ABRIR BIEN LAS PUERTAS AL PROCESO DE TOMA DE DECISIONES

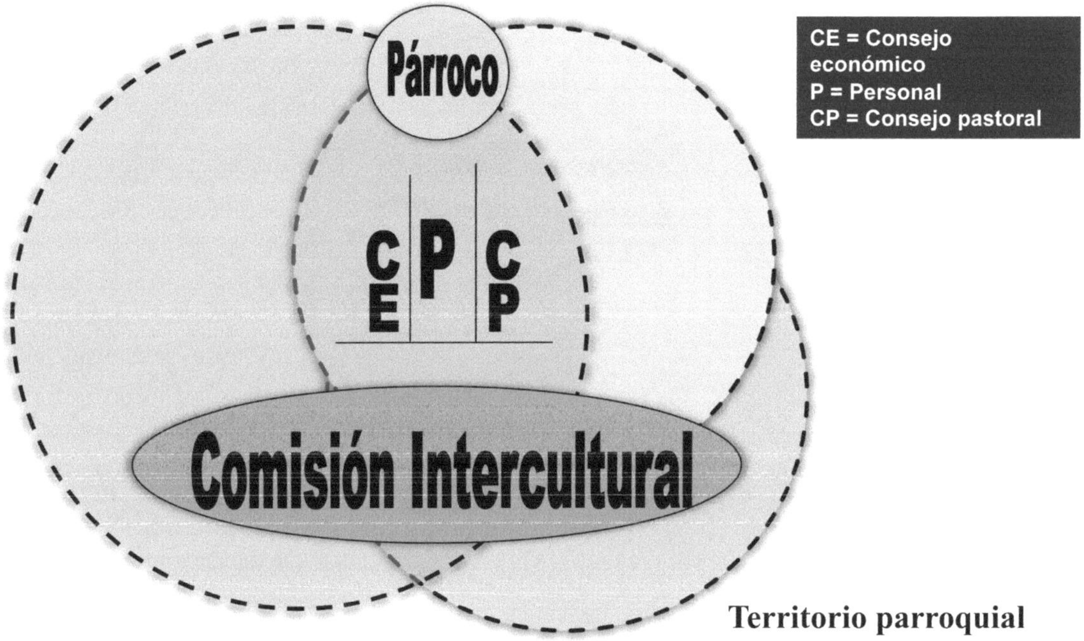

MOVIMIENTO 7—COMPARTIR LOS RECURSOS: FORTALECER EL SENTIDO DE CORRESPONSABILIDAD

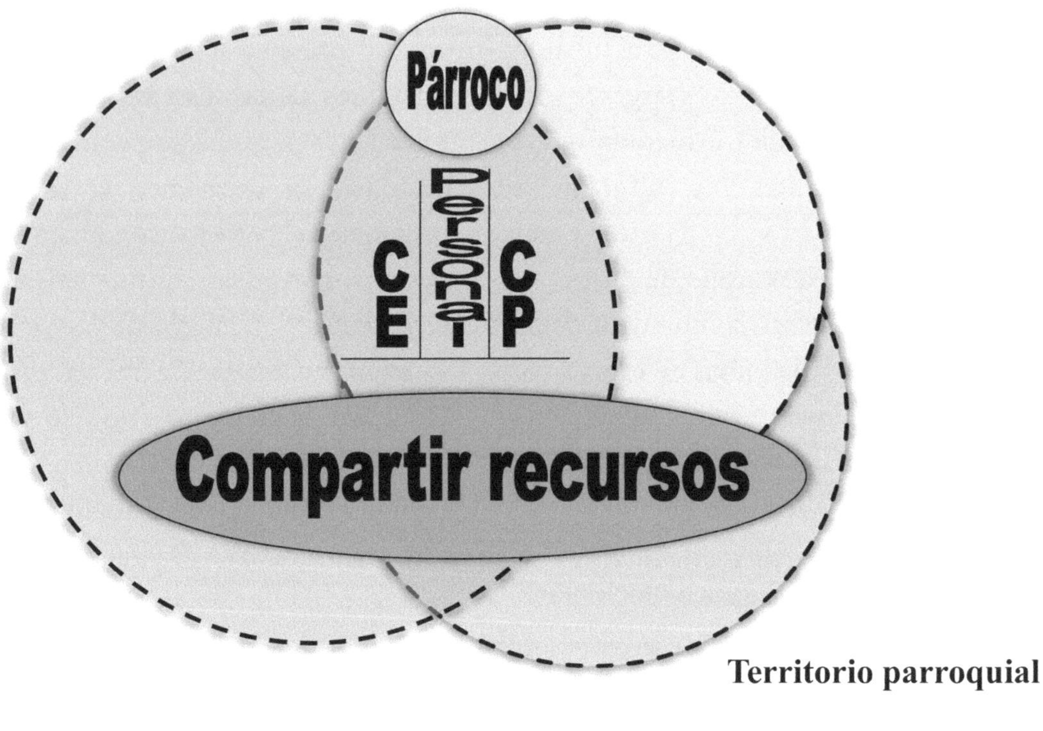

una muestra representativa de las comunidades culturalmente diversas y está equipada con las actitudes, el conocimiento y las destrezas necesarias para servir mejor a toda la comunidad parroquial. El principio de "tener que hacer las cosas tú mismo, pero no hacerlas solo" se aplica al personal que quizás no tenga el manejo de un idioma, como puede ser el vietnamita, pero que sabe cómo involucrar a los líderes de la comunidad vietnamita para que trabajen con él o ella para poder lograr los resultados que se desean de una actividad o un programa concreto. El liderazgo del párroco enfatiza su papel como facilitador que sabe cómo motivar un alto nivel de participación y colaboración y cómo manejar situaciones difíciles a través de un discernimiento orante. Hay un desarrollo significativo en el compartir los recursos materiales por parte de las comunidades vietnamita e hispana, ya que están incluidos en la toma de decisiones de la parroquia en su totalidad. Los líderes de estas dos comunidades ya no están preocupados exclusivamente por el bienestar de sus propias comunidades.

Corresponsabilidad

Movimiento 7: Compartir los recursos

Con este movimiento se logra un sentido de posesión como resultado directo de un proceso inclusivo de toma de decisiones. Las parroquias compartidas que logran este nivel de integración eclesial muestran un liderazgo culturalmente diverso directamente involucrado en el desarrollo del presupuesto parroquial. Las decisiones sobre el uso de las dependencias, el horario de actividades (incluidas misas en distintas lenguas) y la selección de programas concretos toman en consideración las necesidades y aspiraciones de las distintas comunidades presentes en la parroquia. Es muy probable que las parroquias compartidas que están en este nivel de integración eclesial tengan declaraciones de misión que describen a la parroquia como comunidad culturalmente diversa. Lo que sigue son algunos ejemplos:

> *"Somos una comunidad multicultural y diversa unida por nuestra fe en Dios".*
>
> (S. Felipe Benizi, Jonesboro, GA)

> *"Creemos que las diversas culturas en nuestra comunidad son regalos de Dios y, más que asimilarlas, buscamos ser enriquecidos por ellas".*
>
> (S. Francisco de Sales, Holland, MI)

> *"Llevar a todos los pueblos, todas las razas y todos los grupos étnicos a la unión plena con Cristo".*
>
> (Nuestra Señora de Lourdes, Montclair, CA)

> *"Una comunidad multicultural que busca proclamar el Evangelio en nuestros vecindarios y más allá".*
>
> (S. Camilo, Silver Spring, MD)

> *"El aceptar los dones del amor de Dios nos llama a compartir nuestros dones con los demás, incluyendo los pobres, los refugiados, los inmigrantes".*
>
> (Parroquia San José, Amarillo, TX)

El estilo de liderazgo del párroco proporciona pensamiento estratégico, buena administración de los recursos espirituales, humanos y materiales, y orientación para que el liderazgo adquiera una visión clara y una misión para la parroquia en su totalidad. El liderazgo de las distintas comunidades conoce todos los recursos y las necesidades de toda la parroquia y se sienta a la mesa en donde se toman las decisiones sobre el uso de tales recursos. Saben cómo se benefician las distintas comunidades y cómo se lleva a cabo la misión total de la parroquia. Todo esto resulta en un compartir más generoso de los recursos materiales y todos se sienten más inclinados a la práctica de aumentar y regularizar su ofrenda semanal.

Movimiento 8: Lograr la corresponsabilidad

El alto nivel de sentido de posesión conduce a un compartir generoso de tiempo, talento y recursos materiales por parte de todas las comunidades culturales y étnicas involucradas en la vida y misión de una parroquia compartida. Existe un aprecio por los distintos medios y estilos en que las distintas comunidades culturales/étnicas contribuyen a la vida de la parroquia y llevan a cabo la recaudación de fondos. La colaboración es muy intensa a través de las culturas, los ministerios y las actividades y las relaciones personales son muy fuertes entre los miembros del consejo económico, el consejo parroquial y el personal. El papel del párroco es más de apoyo en este movimiento, ya que la visión, la estructura y el liderazgo de la parroquia están establecidos y funcionan bien. Los párrocos a quienes se les consultó para la elaboración de esta guía identificaron las siguientes ideas como muy útiles para lograr un alto nivel de corresponsabilidad en parroquias compartidas:

MOVIMIENTO 8— SEMBRAR Y COSECHAR PLENA CORRESPONSABILIDAD

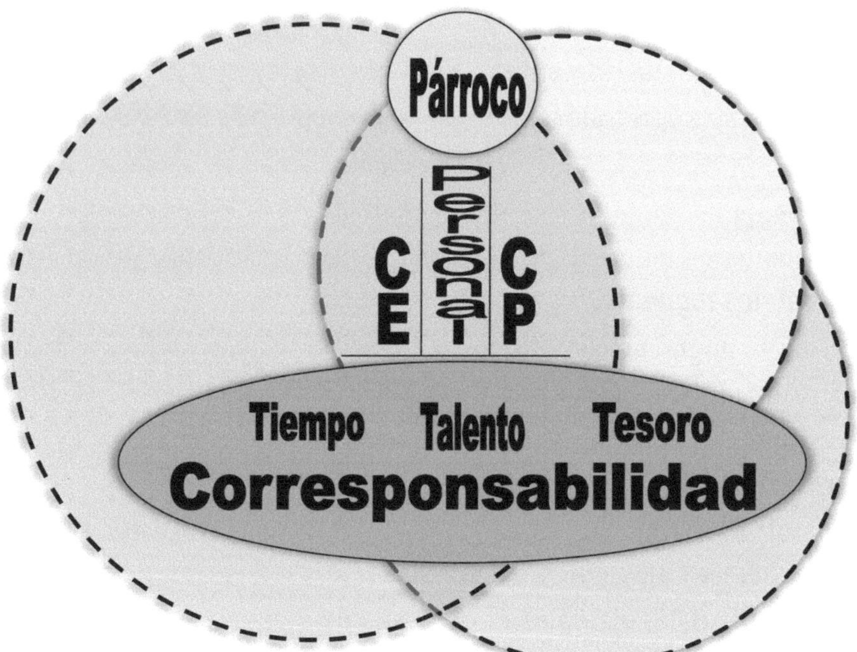

Territorio parroquial

- Permitir a las comunidades de una parroquia que sean distintas juntas
- Desarrollar relaciones cercanas entre los líderes principales de cada comunidad étnica
- Estar abiertos a distintos estilos y medios de corresponsabilidad
- Planificar con las personas, no para las personas
- Encontrar distintos modos para que las comunidades diferentes se apoyen unas a otras en sus luchas
- Enfatizar lo positivo al afirmar a las personas que ya están involucradas en la corresponsabilidad
- Reconocer las necesidades
- Explicar sencillamente y con regularidad cómo se utilizan los recursos
- Evitar comparar a un grupo cultural con otro
- Evitar un pensamiento de esto *o* lo otro abrazando una mentalidad de esto *y* aquello
- Encontrar modos en que la gente pueda simbolizar y ritualizar su corresponsabilidad
- Inventar un lema que todos puedan recordar y recitar
- Desarrollar y capacitar al liderazgo en lugar de hacer las cosas por ellos
- Encontrar modos en que las personas puedan contribuir su trabajo, esfuerzo y sudor
- Enterrar a los muertos y prestar atención al dolor
- Cenar con todos
- Celebrar los éxitos

Movimiento 9: Comunión en misión

Este movimiento no es tanto un lugar de llegada como un nuevo comienzo en la misión de la Iglesia de llevar la Buena Noticia de Jesucristo a toda situación humana. La creciente movilidad humana y los cambios constantes de población exigen que nuestras parroquias sean comunidades acogedoras de discípulos en constante estado de misión. El movimiento también clarifica que la meta de las parroquias compartidas es conducir a los diversos miembros de la parroquia hacia un alto nivel de integración/inclusión eclesial de unos con otros como miembros del único Cuerpo de Cristo. El punto de referencia es el Evangelio, vivido como discípulos de Cristo con la guía del Espíritu Santo. Todas las culturas en la parroquia compartida son transformadas en Cristo y congregadas en una unión más perfecta entre sí y con Dios.

Los párrocos identificaron los siguientes valores y prácticas de la Escritura como ejemplos de cómo debería ser el ministerio en las parroquias compartidas:

- Gn 18:2–8: El recibimiento de Abraham y Sara a los tres forasteros misteriosos en el roble de Mamre.
- Gn 22:17: "Te bendeciré y multiplicaré tu descendencia como las estrellas del cielo y las arenas del mar".
- Lv 19:33–34: "Si un extranjero se instala en la tierra de ustedes, . . .". (*Biblia de América*)
- Rut: Todo el libro ya que reflexiona sobre la salvación a través de un forastero.
- Sir 2:5: "El oro se purifica con el fuego".
- Is 55:1–11: "Todos ustedes, los que tienen sed, vengan por agua . . .".
- Mt 8:20: "El Hijo del hombre no tiene en donde reclinar la cabeza".
- Mt 25:35: "Era forastero y me hospedaron".

MOVIMIENTO 9—LOGRAR UN COMPROMISO TOTAL CON LA MISIÓN DE LA PARROQUIA

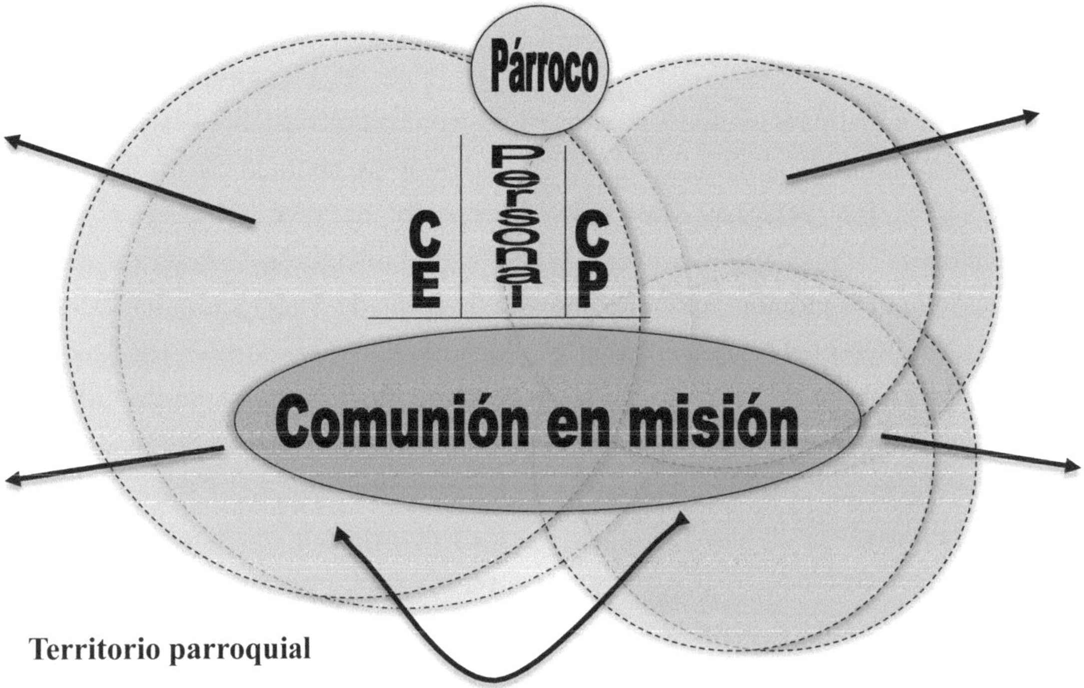

- Hch 2:12: "¿Qué significa esto?". (*Biblia de América*)
- Hch 6:1–7: "Escojan entre ustedes a siete hombres de buena reputación, llenos del Espíritu Santo y de sabiduría, a los cuales encargaremos este servicio . . .".
- Rom 8:31b–39: "Si Dios está a nuestro favor, ¿quién estará en contra nuestra?".
- 1 Cor 12:12–22: "Así como el cuerpo es uno y tiene muchos miembros . . .".
- Gal 3:27–29: "Pues, cuantos han sido incorporados a Cristo por medio del bautismo, se han revestido de Cristo. Ya no existe diferencia entre judíos y no judíos . . .".
- Ap 7:9–10: "Eran individuos de todas las naciones y razas, de todos los pueblos y lenguas. Todos estaban de pie, delante del trono . . .".

Ver las preguntas en la página siguiente para la reflexión al meditar sobre la mejor hoja de ruta para lograr la integración/inclusión eclesial en la parroquia y corresponsabilidad en su comunidad.

Un ejemplo de los nueve movimientos de integración/inclusión eclesial en una parroquia compartida

Las siguientes respuestas vienen de la parroquia San José en Amarillo, Texas. Ilustran la aplicación de los nueve movimientos en el contexto concreto de la parroquia. Además de los nueve movimientos, las respuestas ilustran cómo la parroquia ha manejado el conflicto y logrado sanación en situaciones concretas.

PREGUNTAS PARA LA REFLEXIÓN

1) ¿En cuál de los nueve movimientos sitúa usted su parroquia compartida en este momento de su desarrollo?
2) ¿Qué acciones han ayudado a hacer avanzar este desarrollo?
3) ¿Qué está obstaculizando un mayor desarrollo?
4) ¿Cuáles son algunas de las acciones pastorales que pueden emprender para superar los obstáculos?
5) ¿Hasta qué punto están el párroco y su equipo al unísono en referencia a las metas y el proceso para lograr la integración/inclusión eclesial?
6) ¿Qué podría facilitar la conversación entre el párroco y su equipo para llevar las relaciones interculturales y la colaboración a un nivel más alto?

Las experiencias se incluyen en la guía para generar ideas de posible acción pastoral en parroquias compartidas de todo el país. Se encuentran experiencias parecidas en las otras parroquias que participaron en la consulta. Se escogió San José por la rica variedad de comunidades a las que sirve la parroquia y la creatividad de sus respuestas pastorales.

a) **Salir al encuentro de las personas con espíritu misionero:** La declaración de misión llama a la parroquia a "Dar la bienvenida a todos los hijos de Dios". La Misa dominical se celebra en inglés, español y dinka. Hay una Misa mensual bilingüe (inglés y dinka) y la mayoría de los catequistas, de kínder a escuela secundaria, son bilingües. La comunidad sudanesa proporciona sus propios catequistas bilingües (inglés y dinka).

b) **Practicar la hospitalidad:** Cada tres meses, el liderazgo de la parroquia lleva a cabo una cena de bienvenida para todos los feligreses nuevos. Se ofrece café y *donuts* o pan dulce después de todas las misas dominicales el primer fin de semana del mes. El boletín semanal tiene una sección en español y todo lo que se imprime en el boletín está en ambos idiomas incluso si la información concierne a un solo grupo. El personal es bilingüe. Los anuncios en la Misa se hacen en inglés, español y dinka en la celebración litúrgica común y el párroco es bilingüe —inglés y español— y está aprendiendo dinka.

c) **Proporcionar ministerios culturalmente específicos:** *En la liturgia y la vida de oración*: Todas las celebraciones litúrgicas están a disposición de los fieles en los tres idiomas principales: inglés, español y dinka. Cada grupo de lengua tiene ministros litúrgicos que hablan su idioma y quienes pueden dirigir a la congregación en otras celebraciones litúrgicas no sacramentales o devocionales en su idioma nativo, por ej. Rosarios, vigilias de funeral, novenas, Vía crucis, etc.

En formación de la fe y desarrollo de liderazgo: La formación en la fe de adultos se ofrece en los tres idiomas principales con líderes nativos. Cada grupo tiene su propio programa de formación que refleja su realidad y su nivel de catequización. La parroquia está en proceso de seleccionar candidatos para el diaconado permanente que reflejen cada uno de los tres grupos de idioma.

En servicios sociales y ministerios de justicia social: Cualquier necesidad de servicio de un grupo se comunica a los demás grupos. Por ejemplo, durante las fiestas de Acción de Gracias y Navidad, las familias de los distintos grupos lingüísticos que tienen necesidad reciben la acogida de otra familia u organización parroquial que no es necesariamente del mismo grupo. Los feligreses han ofrecido dinero para funerales para los pobres de la comunidad, o han "adoptado" a niños de familias necesitadas para proveer ropa durante los meses de invierno. Se ofrecen clases de inglés como segundo idioma en la parroquia.

En construir la comunidad a través de culturas y ministerios: La parroquia ofrece celebraciones multiculturales y trilingües para todas las grandes fiestas y celebraciones culturales; un coro trilingüe provee toda la música litúrgica del Triduo y las celebraciones de Navidad. La catequesis se ofrece en todos los eventos religiosos culturales para explicar a los participantes no nativos el significado de la celebración concreta (por ej., Día de los Muertos, Acostamiento del Niño, *Thanksgiving*, Nuestra Señora de Guadalupe, *Memorial Day*, etc.). La parroquia está trabajando para integrar las tres comunidades acogiendo intencionalmente a los otros grupos en celebraciones nativas. Por ejemplo, tienen una Posada todos los años que se celebra en inglés; la comunidad sudanesa danza sus bailes religiosos nativos en honor de la Virgen de Guadalupe; y la Misa del Día de Acción de Gracias se celebra en inglés y en español.

d) **Promover la identidad católica a través de culturas y ministerios:** Los tres grupos lingüísticos están participando en el programa de *Renew, ¿Por qué soy católico?,* cada uno en su propio idioma. El comité organizador tiene representación de las tres comunidades para mantener el sentido de unidad. Se pone énfasis en el hecho de que todos están pasando por el mismo programa que los une como Iglesia Católica.

e) **Manejar las quejas, la falta de comunicación, la desconfianza y la competición entre las comunidades:** La mayoría de las situaciones se discuten abiertamente en la reunión del consejo pastoral. Si es una situación delicada, entonces el párroco la maneja directamente escuchando a las personas/los grupos involucrados.

f) **Promover un sentido de pertenencia a la parroquia entre las comunidades**

que son culturalmente diversas: Los representantes/líderes de los tres grupos lingüísticos tienen llaves de la iglesia y de las salas de reunión, lo cual refleja el hecho de que todos pertenecen y tienen acceso a la iglesia y a los espacios de reunión. Se les pide que llamen a la oficina para programar sus acontecimientos. Todos tienen la misma oportunidad de usar el espacio de reunión.

g) **Compartir historias, proyectos y programas comunes:** Al principio, la comunidad angloparlante pasó por un proceso extenso de planificación que condujo a escribir una declaración de misión y a establecer metas pastorales para la comunidad. La declaración de misión dice: "Somos una familia unida en nuestra fe católica que da la bienvenida a todos los hijos de Dios para continuar el ministerio de Cristo de amar, servir y educar". Esta afirmación preparó a la comunidad para empezar a recibir a otros grupos que Dios enviaba a la parroquia

Desde que se escribió esta declaración de misión, la parroquia ha abierto sus brazos a la Misa en español y la Misa en dinka. Se ha recibido a nuevos bebés a la Iglesia por el sacramento del Bautismo en inglés, español, dinka, croata y creole. Tienen una Misa de unidad al año que ofrece al liderazgo una oportunidad de renovar su compromiso a la alianza original que se escribió, junto con la declaración de misión que los llama a la "unidad en Cristo". El obispo diocesano preside esta Misa. La Misa se celebra en inglés y en español; el párroco proclama el evangelio en dinka; un coro canta en los tres idiomas; y las peticiones se expresan en español, dinka, croata y tagalog, con la respuesta de cada hablante nativo en inglés. Después de la Misa tiene lugar una fiesta comunitaria que incluye a todos los diferente grupos culturales.

La parroquia y su escuela parroquial están trabajando para establecer un instituto cultural y de idiomas para los feligreses. Durante once semanas todos los veranos se ofrecerán clases de lengua: inglés como segundo idioma, español y dinka. Estas clases se ofrecerán simultáneamente, en el mismo edificio y con los descansos al mismo tiempo. Se ofrecerán tres o cuatro clases a los participantes sobre la integración eclesial, basadas en la carta pastoral de los obispos: "Una Iglesia, muchas culturas".

En Pentecostés tienen la celebración anual de la realidad multicultural de la parroquia con un coro trilingüe (inglés, español y dinka). Las oraciones de los fieles se expresan en esos tres idiomas además de croata, tagalog y algunas veces gaélico. El evangelio se proclama en inglés, español, dinka y tagalog. Al final, todos los lectores juntos con el diácono dicen: "El Evangelio del Señor" en inglés.

Todos los fines de semana del mes de mayo hay una coronación de mayo. Cada grupo de lengua tiene la oportunidad de coronar a María en un fin de semana dado. Todos siguen el mismo formato: los representantes de la comunidad se unen al presidente en la procesión de entrada; se canta un canto mariano en el idioma nativo para el canto de entrada; una vez que llegan al santuario, el canto termina y una persona elegida de la comunidad corona a María (a veces un niño y otras veces una anciana o una pareja); la comunidad dirige a la congregación en el rezo del Ave María en su idioma nativo, y el que preside continúa con la Oración de Entrada para la liturgia del domingo. Las diversas comunidades que participan en la coronación de María son: angloparlantes (de ascendencia euroamericana y méxicoamericana), hispana, sudanesa, bosnia, filipina e irlandesa.

h) **Invertir en la formación en la fe y el desarrollo de liderazgo de los líderes y el personal:** Se ha establecido un fondo que ayuda a los representantes de la comunidad a recibir desarrollo de liderazgo y entrenamiento. Como fue establecido recientemente, el enfoque se ha puesto en entrenar a personas en ministerios específicos que se necesitaban. Han tenido a feligreses entrenados en pastoral juvenil centrándose en los adolescentes de la población general y también sirviendo entre los jóvenes latinos/hispanos inmigrantes a través del programa del Instituto Fe y Vida. Otros adultos fueron entrenados en la formación en la fe de los niños, utilizando libros bilingües. Varios representantes de las comunidades que hablan inglés y español fueron enviados a la Conferencia Internacional de Corresponsabilidad Católica para empezar un programa catequético sobre corresponsabilidad en la parroquia.

i) **Incluir una representación culturalmente diversa en los cuerpos de toma de decisión de la parroquia:** El consejo pastoral tiene representación de los grupos principales de lengua inglesa de la parroquia (cuatro euroamericanos y seis méxicoamericanos), así como dos inmigrantes mexicanos y dos personas sudanesas. El consejo económico está compuesto de un euroamericano, tres méxicoamericanos y dos inmigrantes mexicanos. La comunidad sudanesa tiene su propio comité de liderazgo, elegido por la comunidad sudanesa. Los catequistas de la comunidad sudanesa se reúnen con el párroco periódicamente.

j) **Promover el sentido de pertenencia y corresponsabilidad entre todos los feligreses:** Se invita y anima a todos los feligreses a participar en sus propias lenguas en todos los aspectos de la parroquia, incluido el mantenimiento de los locales y el uso de los sobres de ofrenda. El párroco consistentemente da la bienvenida a todos los feligreses a todos estos aspectos de la parroquia. También ha establecido un Comité de Corresponsabilidad (después de recibir entrenamiento en la Conferencia Internacional de Corresponsabilidad Católica) para comenzar a tratar esta área con todos los feligreses.

k) **Facilitar los procesos de toma de decisión:** Se consulta a todos los grupos en el consejo pastoral parroquial. El liderazgo de todos los grupos de la parroquia participa en las reuniones para facilitar las comunicaciones entre cada una de las entidades.

l) **Facilitar la resolución de problemas y de conflictos entre diversas personas y comunidades:** La parroquia se ha hecho más intencional en relación a la integración eclesial. Ha comenzado un proceso de asambleas parroquiales con la participación de las diversas comunidades/familias o grupos en la parroquia. La primera asamblea incluyó una reflexión de cada grupo sobre cómo están viviendo la declaración de misión de la parroquia: "Somos una comunidad de fe católica que da la bienvenida a todos los hijos de Dios para continuar la misión de Cristo de amar, servir y educar". El lema de la parroquia es "Unidad en Cristo". Después de que cada grupo reflexionara sobre cómo están viviendo la declaración de misión, informaron a toda la asamblea parroquial. La discusión y el informe incluían su visión para sí mismos dentro de la declaración de misión.

Los diversos grupos consistían de feligreses veteranos (mayores), la Sociedad del Altar, catequistas, el equipo de pastoral juvenil, líderes adolescentes, *Pastoral Juvenil Hispana*, líderes de la escuela, líderes de la guardería, el equipo de RICA, el liderazgo de la comunidad de habla hispana, el consejo económico, el liderazgo de la comunidad sudanesa, etc. Una religiosa inició con una reflexión espiritual sobre "Ser Iglesia" y la asamblea concluyó con un ritual de compromiso a la "Unidad en Cristo". Después de un breve servicio de oración, un representante de cada grupo se acercó y puso la mano sobre la Piedra de la Unidad como signo de su compromiso con la declaración de misión y con la unidad. En la segunda asamblea parroquial planificada, cada grupo se dirigirá a la asamblea para comunicar en qué punto se ven en la comunidad, lo que los ha ayudado en el proceso de integración y lo que aún necesitan unos de otros. El proceso consistirá de una petición formal, una respuesta formal y un acuerdo (alianza) de unos con otros. Todo esto se hará en un espíritu de oración meditativa y celebración.

m) **Manejar el dolor y facilitar la sanación:** (Es decir, el sentimiento de la comunidad anfitriona bien establecida de que están perdiendo su parroquia, y los recién llegados y huéspedes lidiando con el dolor de dejar atrás su país y su familia).

El párroco se ha reunido con los diversos grupos por separado, para escuchar sus preocupaciones sobre los cambios en la parroquia. También han tenido lugar numerosas reuniones individuales con feligreses. Esto ha incluido reuniones con algunos de los feligreses veteranos de origen euroamericano y méxicoamericano que no se sienten cómodos con que el párroco haga espacio para los recién llegados, y también escuchar a los refugiados sudaneses contar sus historias y las necesidades que plantearían a la parroquia. Todo esto se ha hecho de manera informal, según era necesario, y no siempre planificado.

PREGUNTAS PARA LA REFLEXIÓN

1) ¿Cuáles de estas ideas ha puesto en marcha usted en su parroquia?
2) ¿Qué ideas encuentra útiles para hacer avanzar el proceso de integración/inclusión eclesial en su propia parroquia?
3) ¿Qué se necesitaría para ponerlas en acción?

Ver las preguntas arriba para la reflexión y la acción sobre la experiencia de la parroquia San José.

Situaciones Pastorales y Mejores Prácticas en Parroquias Compartidas

El último componente de la guía presenta situaciones pastorales que han planteado desafíos a los párrocos y sus equipos. Describe cómo han respondido para lograr un resultado positivo. En este sentido, las siguientes respuestas pastorales dan ejemplos de ciertas prácticas óptimas. Cada situación pastoral incluye los siguientes elementos que ayudan a analizar la sabiduría pastoral y el proceso utilizado, de manera que pueda repetirse en aplicaciones pastorales en un futuro en parroquias compartidas:

a) Breve descripción de la situación pastoral
b) Identificación de papeles de cada uno
c) Capacidades interculturales usadas: conocimiento, actitudes y destrezas
d) Intuiciones para la planificación pastoral
e) Principio pastoral

Los párrocos y sus equipos pueden utilizar este proceso como instrumento para evaluar una situación pastoral en su parroquia concreta y buscar elementos clave para lograr resultados positivos. Las situaciones pastorales fueron identificadas por los párrocos que participaron en la consulta y por líderes nacionales de distintas comunidades étnicas y culturales que sirven en parroquias compartidas de Estados Unidos.

Primera situación pastoral: "Misión y bienvenida"

Breve descripción de la situación pastoral

La situación pastoral tiene lugar en Grand Rapids, Michigan, donde una comunidad de Guatemala que hablaba mam (un dialecto maya) se reunía en una casa para orar. La familia que proporcionaba la casa tenía orígenes agricultores y tenía un campo de maíz en la parte de atrás. Los líderes de la comunidad maya invitaron al diácono de la parroquia a visitarlos y él desarrolló una relación con la comunidad. El diácono a su vez invitó al párroco. En unos pocos meses, el grupo de oración había crecido tanto, que habían tenido que añadir un ala a la casa para acoger a la creciente congregación.

Por fin, la parroquia extendió una invitación a usar el auditorio, pero a la comunidad le llevó dos años aceptar la invitación. En unos pocos años, el grupo creció y se dividió en dos grupos con 100 personas cada uno. La parroquia al fin compró una iglesia más grande para acomodar a la creciente comunidad guatemalteca.

Identificación de papeles

Una familia católica decide ser anfitriona de un grupo de católicos mayas que quieren reunirse para orar. Se convierten en puente con la parroquia local y se invita al diácono a conocer a los grupos. El diácono acepta e invita al párroco, consciente de que él es quien toma las decisiones. El párroco pide que el comité social esté disponible para la comunidad maya emergente. Más adelante, el párroco consulta con el consejo parroquial antes de tomar la decisión de invitar a la comunidad maya a ser parte de la parroquia, con espíritu de venida a casa.

Esta experiencia pastoral describe una acción misionera de visitar y dar la bienvenida basada en Mateo 25. Esto le permite al diácono y al párroco escuchar la historia de la comunidad católica maya que vive dentro de los límites de la parroquia. Esta respuesta pastoral se convirtió en un ministerio para la parroquia, coordinado con sensibilidad, tanto cultural como social. Como la comunidad maya se sintió ser bienvenida, estuvo dispuesta a conocer mejor la parroquia y empezó a tener un sentido de conexión y pertenencia.

Capacidades interculturales utilizadas

Conocimiento: Los que están comprometidos en la parte receptora de la comunidad conocen la responsabilidad de la parroquia de cuidar de todos los que viven dentro de los límites de la parroquia. La familia anfitriona, el párroco y el diácono se enteran de la situación de la comunidad maya. El párroco utiliza las estructuras y procesos disponibles en la parroquia para decidir dar la bienvenida a la comunidad maya para que comparta en la vida y misión de la parroquia en un espíritu de regreso al hogar.

Destrezas: El poder de persuasión, tanto por parte del diácono que llamó la atención del párroco sobre la situación como por parte del párroco que llevó la respuesta a la comunidad maya y a la comunidad más amplia. Supervisión.

Actitudes: Apertura a nuevas posibilidades. Tomar riesgos. Ir más allá de las zonas más cómodas. Generosidad, hospitalidad y solidaridad que demuestran todas las personas involucradas.

Intuición de planificación pastoral

Se identifica la necesidad escuchando y observando con sensibilidad pastoral; a través de la consulta con el equipo pastoral y los centros de toma de decisiones; a través de la supervisión del desarrollo del ministerio; a través de situar el ministerio en el contexto parroquial, el análisis de recursos, la distribución y la supervisión; y a través de un trabajo de equipo.

Principio pastoral

Encontrar a las personas allá donde estén desde un espíritu de misión.

Segunda situación pastoral: "Dos parroquias que comparten el mismo párroco"

Breve descripción de la situación pastoral

La situación pastoral incluye a dos parroquias católicas predominantemente negras que se encuentran a cinco millas una de la otra. Compartían una historia y herencia comunes, pero nunca se habían unido para hacer cosas juntos. Una parroquia es de origen creole y la otra de origen afroamericano. Debido a la escasez de sacerdotes en la diócesis, se pidió que las dos parroquias compartieran un párroco. El párroco de la parroquia creole fue asignado a la parroquia afroamericana, mientras que el párroco de la parroquia afroamericana fue asignado a otra parroquia de la diócesis. Los feligreses de la parroquia creole estaban satisfechos con el cambio, ya que se quedarían con el mismo párroco. Pero los feligreses de la parroquia afroamericana rechazaron la idea de compartir un sacerdote con la otra parroquia.

El párroco nombrado para las dos parroquias vio subir la tensión debido a la nueva situación y decidió formar un equipo de reconciliación de diez miembros con representantes de las dos parroquias, para que lo ayudaran a navegar las difíciles aguas del dolor y el cambio. El párroco facilitó un retiro sobre el tema de la reconciliación con su nuevo equipo, seguido por seminarios sobre la universalidad de la Iglesia como un solo Cuerpo de Cristo, que se ofrecieron a los miembros de las dos parroquias. Estas dos experiencias compartidas de reconciliación y de la misión de la Iglesia prepararon el campo para un encuentro con miembros de ambas parroquias para expresar sus preocupaciones y aspiraciones y discernir el camino a tomar. El proceso se cerró con la celebración del sacramento de la Reconciliación. El proceso de reconciliación que facilitó el párroco permitió a los miembros de las dos parroquias escucharse y compartir historias, perspectivas y preocupaciones sobre la nueva situación pastoral. El proceso acercó a las dos parroquias y las puso en la misma perspectiva sobre el futuro bajo un solo párroco. Las parroquias ahora comparten programas de educación religiosa, maestros y un equipo pastoral común que ayuda al párroco a desarrollar planes pastorales y programas para las dos parroquias.

Identificación de papeles

El obispo tomó la difícil decisión de que un párroco asumiera la responsabilidad de dos parroquias distintas debido a la situación de escasez de sacerdotes. A pesar de la cercanía geográfica, los miembros de las dos parroquias en cuestión no se conocían y no habían trabajado juntos nunca, lo cual aumentaba la complejidad de la situación. El párroco nombrado proporcionó un liderazgo muy acertado escuchando las preocupaciones de los feligreses, designando un equipo representativo y poniendo en marcha un proceso eficaz de reconciliación. Los diez miembros del equipo de reconciliación trabajaron bien con el párroco y con sus comunidades parroquiales respectivas, y así pusieron el tono para un proceso de reconciliación orante y con éxito. Aprender más sobre la identidad católica y la misión de la Iglesia les dio un renovado sentido de unidad en Cristo. El liderazgo de ambas parroquias está dispuesto a compartir un programa de educación religiosa y a colaborar en otras actividades pastorales.

Capacidades interculturales utilizadas

Conocimiento: El párroco entiende muy bien su papel como unificador y es capaz de ayudar a los miembros de ambas parroquias a entender mejor el significado de la identidad católica y de la misión de la Iglesia. El proceso de reconciliación promovió el conocimiento y entendimiento mutuo entre todos los involucrados, pasando así más allá de estereotipos y prejuicios.

Actitudes: El sentido de apertura del párroco para implicar el liderazgo de ambas parroquias ayuda a crear un espacio de seguridad y confianza entre los diez miembros del equipo de reconciliación. Hay apertura a nuevas posibilidades, a la toma de riesgo y a pasar más allá de las zonas de comodidad con paciencia, perseverancia, coraje y humildad. Todos tienen la oportunidad de, juntos, participar y aportar ideas, opiniones, recomendaciones y soluciones. Cuando todos están involucrados, hay más oportunidades de llevar los asuntos a una conclusión positiva.

Destrezas: La capacidad de crear un equipo bien representado que desarrolle un proceso de reconciliación y lo facilite con éxito. Escucharse con apertura y tomar decisiones en el contexto de la oración. La capacidad de discutir y dialogar, el poder de la negociación y la capacidad de ceder para llegar a un acuerdo y para comunicar los asuntos en juego en términos sencillos y hacer los procesos de reconciliación y toma de decisiones exitoso.

Intuición de planificación pastoral

Identificar los asuntos y crear un equipo representativo para trabajar con el párroco desde el principio. Desarrollar un proceso que garantice un alto grado de participación y oportunidades para compartir, análisis de temas, oración, conseguir nuevo conocimiento y establecer un proceso de toma de decisiones inclusivo que conduzca a la unidad y la colaboración.

Principio pastoral

Pasar del lenguaje de "nosotros-ellos" al lenguaje de "nosotros".

Tercera situación pastoral: "Compartir los recursos que les pertenecen a todos"

Breve descripción de la situación

Bajo el liderazgo del párroco, una parroquia urbana compuesta mayoritariamente de estadounidenses y afroamericanos decidió dar la bienvenida a nuevos inmigrantes católicos hispanos, ya que se dieron cuenta de que estaban viviendo dentro de los límites de la parroquia. Una vez que se estableció la liturgia dominical en español, el número de hispanos que asistía a esa Misa creció muy rápidamente y las peticiones de otros servicios pastorales empezaron a emerger, e iban de educación religiosa y grupos de oración a servicios sociales, entre otras cosas. La actitud de acogida hacia la nueva comunidad se encontró con una crisis cuando empezaron a llegarle al párroco quejas de la comunidad que había estado allí más tiempo sobre el cuidado de las dependencias. La percepción de que los hispanos no estaban cuidando bien de las dependencias llevó a algunos feligreses a sugerir que el nuevo hall no debería estar disponible para esa comunidad y que se debería elaborar algún tipo de acuerdo firmado para asegurarse de que los hispanos sabían cómo cuidar de las dependencias que ya estaban utilizando. El resentimiento crecía por los dos lados a medida que los hispanos empezaron a sentirse rechazados y tratados injustamente.

Como el consejo parroquial no tenía en aquel momento miembros hispanos, el párroco decidió formar un pequeño grupo de feligreses muy bien seleccionados, representantes de las comunidades euroamericana, afroamericana e hispana, con el único propósito de evaluar las dependencias parroquiales y desarrollar criterios para su uso y cuidado. El pequeño grupo empezó por evaluar las dependencias y elaborar recomendaciones de reparaciones y mejoras. Como segundo paso, el grupo identificó los pasos necesarios para cuidar bien y consistentemente todas las dependencias, incluido el nuevo hall y desarrolló un calendario que era claro y accesible a todos los feligreses. Una vez que el grupo completó su trabajo, hizo una recomendación formal al párroco para que lo revisara y aprobara. Se informó a todos los feligreses sobre el compromiso de todos con la buena administración de las dependencias parroquiales y se hicieron carteles en inglés y español para recordar a los que las utilizaran los pasos necesarios para *leave the place better than they found it / dejar el lugar mejor de lo que estaba*. El uso compartido responsable de las dependencias y el buen cuidado de ellas, por parte de todos, mejoró significativamente como resultado de este proceso.

Identificación de papeles

El párroco escuchó las quejas legítimas sobre la importancia de cuidar bien de las dependencias parroquiales. También estaba muy consciente de las actitudes poco acogedoras potenciales y del conflicto que podría apoderarse de las comunidades y de las personas, en especial sobre el nuevo hall, lo que podría convertirse en símbolo de división entre los que estaban "dentro" y los de fuera. Los representantes de las tres comunidades —afroamericanos, euroamericanos e hispanos— fueron bien seleccionados por el párroco y entendieron muy bien que la misión del grupo no era que una comunidad le dijera a la otra qué hacer, o cómo hacerlo. Más bien, se trataba de promover un sentido común de posesión de las dependencias y, por lo tanto, de un buen cuidado de ellas. Esto ayudó a lograr un renovado sentido de unidad de manera que las tres comunidades diferentes de la parroquia tienen acceso al proceso de toma de decisiones. Todos los feligreses se sintieron bien acerca de cuidar del nuevo hall, porque les pertenecía a todos.

Capacidades interculturales utilizadas

Conocimiento: El párroco muestra un sólido entendimiento de la corresponsabilidad y de la importancia de que todos los feligreses tengan un sentido de posesión en referencia a los locales parroquiales. El conocimiento de cómo lidian con el conflicto las diversas culturas y cómo toman decisiones también fue útil para reunir al grupo que evaluó las condiciones de los locales e hizo recomendaciones para cuidar bien de ellas.

Actitudes: Hubo apertura por parte del párroco para escuchar las quejas de la gente y confiar en que podría salir una situación positiva de la crisis inminente. Los líderes en el grupo designado y el personal también estuvieron abiertos y dispuestos a involucrarse unos con otros sin caer en el juego de las acusaciones mutuas o en una lucha por el poder.

Destrezas: Buena escucha y una buena comunicación intercultural entre las tres comunidades distintas; un uso eficaz de las destrezas de resolución de conflictos; dinámica de grupos y procesos de toma de decisión.

Intuición de planificación pastoral

Desarrollo de un grupo con un objetivo específico, designado por el párroco e investido de autoridad para hacer recomendaciones. El proceso de toma de decisiones fue transparente y cada comunidad se sintió bien representada. Así, todo el mundo aceptó las orientaciones para el buen cuidado de los locales.

Principio pastoral

Un proceso inclusivo de toma de decisiones a menudo conduce a un sentido de posesión común.

Cuarta situación pastoral: "Desarrollo espiritual y de liderazgo"

Breve descripción de la situación pastoral

La parroquia era muy multicultural y había una cantidad considerable de formación espiritual que ya estaba tomando lugar dentro de los distintos grupos lingüísticos. Sin embargo, no había un programa intercultural en el que la gente pudiera desarrollarse tanto espiritualmente como como líderes. La parroquia ofreció una oportunidad de participar en un programa de 14 semanas titulado *Liderazgo servidor*. En las reuniones semanales, el grupo exploró áreas como la autoconciencia, empoderamiento, transparencia y construcción de la comunidad a medida que desarrollaban un estilo creativo y respetuoso de *liderazgo servidor*. El programa creó un espacio para que personas de muchas culturas distintas pudiera compartir lo significaba cada tema para ellos desde el punto de vista de su cultura e historia, y de ampliar su perspectiva al compartir con otros y en la lectura de los pensamientos de autoridades respetadas en el área de la espiritualidad y el liderazgo. En el curso de esos tres meses, se formaron relaciones y se creó un sentido de comunidad. La mayoría de los participantes pasarían a servir en posiciones de liderazgo en la parroquia, llevando con ellos su perspectiva ampliada, lo cual sería importante especialmente para quienes, por último, pasarían a servir en un consejo pastoral multicultural.

Para algunos, la experiencia fue tan fuerte que quisieron compartirla con otros. Estaban preparados como facilitadores y durante los siguientes años guiaron a otros a través del mismo proceso que tanta vida les había dado a ellos mismos.

Al ver los frutos de este programa, años más tarde, el párroco decidió que podría beneficiar a su personal multicultural y así, durante un año, los sacerdotes y el personal laico participaron en el programa para profundizar su comprensión mutual y lo que significa ser líder servidor.

Identificación de papeles

El párroco ve la necesidad de proporcionar oportunidades de crecimiento espiritual y desarrollo de liderazgo para líderes parroquiales de diversas comunidades culturales en su parroquia. Identifica *Liderazgo servidor* como programa que cubre bien ambas áreas y decide hacer la inversión para traer el programa a la parroquia. Los líderes de las diversas comunidades culturales responden bien a la invitación del párroco a participar en el programa y tienen una experiencia muy buena. El párroco decide proporcionar la misma oportunidad a los sacerdotes y personal laico de la parroquia.

Capacidades interculturales utilizadas

Conocimiento: El párroco sabe que los líderes parroquiales están preparados para crecer espiritualmente y para desarrollar más destrezas de liderazgo. Identifica un buen recurso para proporcionar la formación necesaria. El párroco también sabe cómo invitar con éxito y asegurar la participación de líderes de las diversas comunidades culturales de la parroquia.

Actitudes: Apertura a crecer espiritualmente y a desarrollar nuevas destrezas por parte del párroco, los líderes parroquiales y el personal; apertura a compartir perspectivas culturales sobre el contenido del programa; y apertura a desarrollar un sentido de comunidad entre los miembros culturalmente diversos. Inversión generosa de tiempo, talento y recursos para la formación.

Destrezas: Consulta e investigación para identificar el programa más adecuado. Destrezas organizativas para coordinar el programa de entrenamiento en términos de lugares, tiempos, hospitalidad y recursos relacionados. El propio programa mejoró las destrezas de los participantes en términos de autoconciencia, empoderamiento, transparencia y construcción de la comunidad a medida que desarrollaban un estilo de liderazgo servidor creativo y respetuoso.

Intuición de planificación pastoral

Una fuerza de liderazgo cualificada es uno de los mejores tesoros para el desarrollo y puesta en marcha de estrategias e iniciativas pastorales. También construye comunidad y un sentido de pertenencia.

Principio pastoral

Defensa incondicional de la formación y desarrollo de liderazgo dentro de cada comunidad cultural y étnica a través de experiencias comunes.

Quinta situación pastoral: "Planificación estratégica parroquial"

Breve descripción de la situación pastoral

En 2003–2004 se dio un proceso de planificación estratégica en la parroquia para desarrollar un plan pastoral para los tres años siguientes. Unas cuarenta personas que ya estaban implicadas en el ministerio se reunieron bajo la dirección de un facilitador de la diócesis. Aunque la parroquia era inmigrante en un 75 por ciento, la participación fue mayoritariamente euroamericana. Se invitó a los participantes a soñar y se les preguntó: "¿Qué queremos ver que ocurra en esta parroquia en tres años?". El gran grupo identificó un número de áreas y luego se invitó a la gente a ir a su área de interés y desarrollar un plan de acción. Algunas cosas muy buenas surgieron del proceso, como un ministerio multicultural para jóvenes adultos, un ministerio juvenil renovado, un nuevo ministerio centrado en temas de justicia y paz, y algunas renovaciones del edificio del templo.

En 2008, motivado en el deseo de que el proceso fuera más colaborativo y consultivo, se usó un modelo distinto titulado Prácticas Óptimas para las Parroquias un programa que permite a la parroquia llevar a cabo un autoestudio para "medirse" frente a las cien parroquias más vibrantes en las siete áreas clave de la vida parroquial, como la oración y el culto, la vida familiar y pastoral, la evangelización y la corresponsabilidad. Cada área tenía una serie detallada de preguntas en las que se pedía a los participantes que calificaran a su parroquia en un área concreta: "¿Hicieron algo muy bien, aceptable, rara vez o no en absoluto?".

Se llevó a un asesor para ayudar con el proceso y se sacó un núcleo del consejo parroquial para manejar el proceso. Se entrenó a facilitadores en los tres principales idiomas para llevar a cabo estas distintas sesiones escucha de auto-estudio. Algunas de las personas invitadas a participar estaban ya implicadas en el ministerio, y otras no. Cuando se recopilaron los resultados, se descubrió que en muchas áreas la calificación para una pregunta concreta dependía de qué grupo lingüístico contestaba. Por ejemplo, cuando se pedía que calificaran la hospitalidad en la Misa, los africanos franco parlantes, con un ministerio de hospitalidad muy desarrollado, la calificaron de alta, mientras que los latinos que estaban en proceso de formar un ministerio la calificaron cerca del medio y los que asistían a misas en inglés la calificaron de baja. Por otro lado, en la categoría de justicia y paz, los euroamericanos calificaron los esfuerzos de la parroquia como "altos", los franco parlantes "algo" y los hispanos "rara vez". En otras muchas preguntas, la respuesta dependía de qué grupo lingüístico contestaba.

Los resultados de lo que se hacía bien o no tan bien fueron publicados en la página web y luego llevados a siete reuniones abiertas que se realizaron en un período de siete semanas. Cada reunión se centró en una de las siete áreas. Todos los miembros de la parroquia fueron invitados a participar en tantas reuniones como quisieran. El grupo se reunía para la oración y luego se dividía en tres grupos por lenguas para recomendar, dados los resultados, lo que deberían ser las metas en esa área concreta por los próximos tres años. Estas recomendaciones se llevaban al plenario y se compartían para que se pudieran entender las razones de cada grupo. Luego el plenario hacía sus recomendaciones. Cientos de personas participaron en esta fase del proceso y todos crecieron en la comprensión de las otras comunidades lingüísticas y de sus talentos y desafíos.

Cuando se acabaron las siete reuniones, las recomendaciones pasaron al consejo pastoral multicultural y ellos identificaron las prioridades, escogieron las metas y desarrollaron un plan de acción con líneas de tiempo y responsabilidades. Se publicaron los resúmenes en el boletín y el plan, de 74 páginas, se puso permanentemente en el sitio web de la parroquia.

Como el proceso fue consultivo en todos los niveles, había una mayor comprensión de lo que la parroquia estaba tratando de lograr, un sentido de misión de la parroquia más acentuado y una mayor comprensión de su diversidad y complejidad y, al fin, más sentido de posesión del plan.

Principio pastoral

Planifica con las personas, no para las personas.

Ejercicio: Identifique su propia práctica óptima

Siguiendo el guión que se utiliza en las cinco situaciones pastorales, que mostraba prácticas concretas, identifique una situación pastoral en su propia parroquia que fue manejada de tal manera que la respuesta se podría considerar una práctica óptima.

a) Breve descripción de la situación pastoral
b) Identificación de papeles
c) Capacidades interculturales utilizadas: conocimiento, actitudes, destrezas
d) Intuición para la planificación pastoral
e) Principio pastoral

Conclusión

La vida parroquial es el contexto privilegiado en que los católicos experimentan un encuentro personal y comunitario con Cristo. Es también el hogar espiritual en que los fieles desarrollan un sentido de pertenencia en la Iglesia y donde se involucran en ministerios de servicio mutuo y a la comunidad más amplia. El surgimiento de miles de *parroquias compartidas* en las últimas décadas es una respuesta pastoral a un enorme cambio de población que está teniendo lugar en diócesis de todo el país. Las parroquias compartidas son también un *signo de los tiempos*, que llama a los católicos de distintas razas, culturas y etnias a experimentar de nuevo el espíritu de Pentecostés, para que puedan oírse y entenderse unos a otros, movidos por el mismo espíritu del amor, nutridos en la misma mesa Eucarística del Señor.

Sin embargo, construir la unidad en la diversidad exige actitudes, conocimiento y destrezas concretas. También requiere que se tenga un claro y profundamente eclesial entendimiento de lo que se quiere lograr en nuestras parroquias compartidas, y cómo lo queremos hacer. Estamos agradecidos de que el espíritu de unidad y de amor pastoral ha inspirado a muchos párrocos y a sus equipos a lograr un alto nivel integración/inclusión eclesial entre los miembros de diversas culturas en sus parroquias compartidas.

Las historias, los principios pastorales y las recomendaciones prácticas incluidas en esta guía constituyen un gran recurso para miles de párrocos a quienes se ha confiado el cuidado pastoral en parroquias compartidas y para otros que se podrían encontrar sirviendo en una parroquia compartida en el futuro. La guía es también útil para el personal y los líderes parroquiales que colaboran con el párroco en la maravillosa pero difícil tarea de construir unidad en la diversidad. Junto con los ejemplos prácticos y las intuiciones, la guía proporciona una metodología para entender el proceso de sensibilidad intercultural y de integración sana. Esta metodología se interpreta a través de una espiritualidad de ministerio y un sentido de identidad católica que se basa en la Escritura que ha inspirado y guiado el trabajo de muchos párrocos de parroquias compartidas y sus equipos.

Somos muy conscientes de que la obra de la Nueva Evangelización se está llevando a cabo en las parroquias compartidas de una manera única, a medida que nos convertimos en misioneros unos de otros, y honramos la presencia de Cristo en las distintas culturas. Que cada vez estemos más unidos en la Mesa Eucarística del Señor en nuestras parroquias y otras instituciones católicas; y que hagamos eco en nuestras vidas a la oración de Cristo por todos nosotros: **"PARA QUE TODOS SEAN UNO".**